tapas fantásticas
appetizers with a Spanish Flair

Bob & Coleen Simmons

BRISTOL PUBLISHING ENTERPRISES, INC.
San Leandro, California

Printed in Singapore through Global Interprint.

ISBN 1-55867-233-8

Design: *Shanti L. Nelson*
Photography: *À La Carte Digital Studios*
Food styling: *Bob and Coleen Simmons*
Project editor: *Lisa M. Tooker*

www.bristolcookbooks.com

table of
contents

what are tapas?

Smoked Salmon & Cucumber Tartlets, page 98

Tapas are small, flavorful dishes that are a very important part of Spain's social and cultural lifestyle. The Spanish love to talk, eat and drink, and tapas bars and restaurants provide a convenient place to do all three.

The tapas tradition, which has been developed and refined over the last hundred years, started with innkeepers providing a small nibble to accompany a glass of wine. The food was often full-flavored and salty. Foods like almonds, olives, a piece of cheese or a thin slice of ham were served. These morsels were probably intended to stimulate the desire for another glass of wine. Tapas in Spanish means cover, and the nibble was often served on a small plate, which was carried to the customer balanced on top of a wineglass.

Today, tapas are very popular and are served all over Spain. Many tapas bars acquire a reputation and following for their own unique specialties. An evening of fun may include a stop at several different places for a small plate or two, and another glass of wine before going on to dinner. Tapas bars are as varied as their clientele. Some bars are very small with no seating, and offer a limited tapas selection like a tortilla and a house special or two. Some of the more elaborate tapas establishments are found in Seville and Madrid where a restaurant or bar may have as many as 40 different tapas selections. The traditional beverage served with tapas is dry sherry, but young fruity red or white wines, beer, sangria or even cocktails complement a broad range of tapas dishes.

Tapas customs have spread around the globe, and you can find tapas bars and restaurants in most U.S. cities. Tapas originally filled the long gaps between mealtimes in Spain; today, an assortment of tapas dishes can provide a delicious alternative to dinner.

Beef & Potato Empanadas, page 121

preparing

tapas

Spanish cuisine is flavorful, refined, spicy but not firey hot. Moorish foods and spices, as well as New World tomatoes, potatoes and peppers have all been assimilated into Spanish dishes. The ingredients for most of the tapas recipes can be found in U.S. supermarkets. A list of recommended substitutes for some harder-to-find Spanish ingredients is also provided in *the tapas pantry*, pages 8-15.

Tapas are easy to prepare and can readily be made at home. Many tapas are better when cooked a day in advance and then served at room temperature, or reheated just before guests arrive.

Tapas are party foods! Serve a couple of tapas with drinks for a cocktail party or as appetizers before a barbecue. Or serve several different tapas and make them your main meal. Tapas can be as simple or as elaborate as you desire. Adapt the Spanish custom of leisurely eating and drinking and make cooking tapas fun!

the
tapas pantry

Simple tapas can be assembled at a moment's notice from ingredients in the refrigerator or on the pantry shelf, or picked up at your local grocery store. Look for olives, cubes of cheese, cubes or slices of ham, caperberries and pickles; ready-to-eat sausage like pepperoni, salami and summer sausage; or hard-boiled eggs; nuts such as roasted almonds, hazelnuts and cashews; or other items like roasted red peppers, tins of tuna, sardines, anchovies, smoked clams or smoked oysters.

All good cooking starts with high-quality ingredients. The information in this chapter will help you to select ingredients for your next tapas adventure.

anchovies

Many people claim that they don't like anchovies. This may be the result of their experience with salty, dried-out bits of anchovies found served as toppings on pizza. Anchovies are available preserved in salt, oil-packed in jars and tins and as a paste. When finely chopped, anchovies can add complexity and flavor to a dish without tasting overly fishy.

To prepare anchovies preserved in salt, rinse the surface salt from the anchovy under running water. Pull off the head and, with a sharp knife, make a shallow cut down the backbone. Remove one fillet from the bone and then pull the bone from the other fillet. Rinse the fillets again under running water and place in a shallow bowl in one layer. Cover with milk or water and allow to marinate for one hour. Drain, pat dry with paper towels and use as you would anchovies packed in oil.

Anchovies in oil come both in jars and the familiar two-ounce tin. Those in jars are usually higher quality. Rinsing oil-packed anchovies under cool running water removes some of the saltiness and gives the anchovies a fresher taste.

Anchovy paste packaged in a tube is very easy to use. A small amount in a recipe adds saltiness and brings out other flavors.

capers

Capers are the flower bud of a hardy plant that grows in the Mediterranean region. They range in size from a pea to the tip of a little finger. Usually packed in vinegar, capers should be well drained and rinsed in cool water before using. Capers are also preserved in salt, and should be rinsed and soaked in cool water for a few minutes to remove some saltiness and refresh their flavor.

Caperberries are the fruit that develops after the bud flowers. They are about the size of a small olive, have a long stem and are packed in vinegar. They are found in jars and in the deli section of some supermarkets. You can skewer them to create a *banderilla,* page 28, or use them in salads. They are also currently a popular replacement for the olive in a martini.

cheese

Spain produces many wonderful cheeses. Most are at least partially made from sheep's or goat's milk. Three cheeses often found in the U.S. are manchego, cabrales and mahón. Traditional manchego is made from sheep's milk. It can be identified by the basket-weave pattern on the side of the cheese wheel. Young manchego is mild and creamy, and aged manchego has a firmer texture and a more assertive flavor. Both are delicious for eating and cooking. Older manchego is often grated and added to dishes like Italian Parmesan. Aged manchego is often thinly sliced and served with membrillo or quince paste, and served as tapas or at the end of a meal with a glass of red wine. A young Italian pecorino Romano can be substituted for manchego.

Cabrales is a creamy blue sheep's milk cheese that is wrapped in chestnut leaves before aging. It is creamier than Roquefort and milder than Gorgonzola, either of which can be substituted for cabrales. Mahón is similar to Dutch Gouda, which makes a wonderful substitute. Spanish goat cheeses are not often imported into the U.S., but French or domestic make good substitutes.

garlic

The Romans brought garlic to all the Mediterranean countries they conquered and Spain has loved it ever since. It is used raw, rubbed over toasted bread slices, and added as an important ingredient in many cooked sauces and dishes. Fresh garlic is preferred over dried powders and salts. Buy firm, plump bulbs and store them in a cool, dark place. Cut fresh cloves in half lengthwise, and if there is a green shoot running from root to stem, remove it before slicing or mincing since it tends to be very bitter. Mincing or finely chopping garlic releases more pungent and assertive flavors than thinly slicing the cloves. Roasting whole heads of garlic produces a mellow sweet garlic paste that pairs wonderfully with potatoes, tomatoes, eggplant or toast.

ham

Ham is frequently used in tapas. The most flavorful is the Spanish jamon serrano, which is salted and cured in a manner similar to Italian prosciutto. It is very thinly sliced with the grain, and served on a slice of toasted bread or wrapped around a ripe fig. Spanish serrano ham is becoming more available in the U.S., but is expensive. More commonly used are imported or domestic prosciutto brands, which are good substitutions for serrano hams. Other cooked hams such as jamon York are often used, or substitute Black Forest ham or Virginia baked ham.

onions

The large yellow, Spanish onions have a high sugar content, and turn sweet and mellow when slowly cooked in a little olive oil. They lend flavor to a wide variety of tapas. Shallots are milder and sweeter than onions, and add balance to sauces and piquant vinaigrettes. The familiar green onion is used both raw or slightly cooked.

almonds

Almonds simply roasted and lightly salted make a delicious snack and are frequently served as tapas. They can also be ground and used as a thickener for sauces or as an ingredient in desserts. Roasting your own almonds will produce nuts with a better, fresher taste than buying them already roasted.

Almonds can be roasted and eaten without removing the brown skin. If you want to remove the brown skin blanch almonds by placing them in a bowl and covering with boiling water for 5 minutes. Drain and slip the skins off.

Raw almond slices, slivers and whole almonds should be toasted to bring out their nutty flavor before use in recipes. Heat oven to 275°. Place nuts on a cookie sheet and bake, shaking the pan often, until almonds are lightly browned. Whole almonds will take 30 to 35 minutes; slivered and sliced nuts should be checked after 10 minutes. Remove from the oven when you smell a wonderful toasty aroma.

pine nuts

Pine nuts are delicious when lightly toasted. They can be eaten alone, added to a finished dish, sprinkled over salads or incorporated into desserts. To toast pine nuts, heat the oven to 275°. Place the nuts on a cookie sheet and bake until lightly browned, about 5 to 7 minutes. Shake the pan often, and watch carefully because they burn easily. Pine nuts can also be toasted in a dry nonstick skillet over low heat. Shake the pan often until the pine nuts are golden brown.

bell peppers

Spanish food is robust and full-flavored, but not as chile-laden as Mexican or Southwestern foods. Green, yellow and particularly red peppers that are roasted, peeled and marinated in a little olive oil and vinegar are used extensively. Pimiento peppers are large heart-shaped, thick-walled red peppers with a wonderful sweet flavor. This pepper is commonly used for stuffing green olives. Pimientos are found fresh in some specialty markets or farmers' markets, but more often are found processed in cans or jars.

Roasting your own peppers is easy. Line a shallow baking pan with foil for easy cleanup, and place a small rack on the foil. Preheat broiler. Wash and dry the peppers and place them on a rack. Broil about 8 inches from heat source, turning peppers as they roast so all sides are slightly blackened. Remove peppers from broiler, place in a bowl and cover with foil, or wrap each pepper in foil. Steam for 10 to 15 minutes. After steaming, the pepper skins slip off easily. Do not rinse under cold water. Remove seeds and core. Store in an airtight container in the refrigerator until ready to use.

sausage

Spain has a wonderful variety of cured pork sausages. Chorizo, an air-dried sausage, is made of pork, cumin, garlic and powdered chiles. It can be found at Spanish markets and in some meat shops. It is sold when young and moist, or aged and drier. Slice it and eat it raw or incorporate it into cooked dishes. Do not substitute Mexican chorizo, which is a different product and must be removed from the casing and cooked before using. If chorizo is not available, substitute Italian pepperoni, soppressa or Portuguese linguica. We have provided a recipe for a homemade chorizo that, while not at all authentic, has some of the flavor and character of the real thing.

salt cod

The Spanish developed a taste for *bacalao*, as they call salt cod, long before refrigeration was available. Cod was salted and dried in the cold, dry climate of the North Atlantic and then imported into Spain. Salt cod must be soaked for a day in several changes of water to leach out the salt. It is then boiled to soften before it's used in a recipe. Salt cod pairs especially well with potatoes.

The most manageable way to buy salt cod is in one-pound wooden boxes. The fish has already been boned and skinned and the pieces are fairly uniform in thickness. If buying a whole unpackaged piece, choose a thicker one. The thin end pieces tend to resist softening when soaked.

saffron

Known as the world's most expensive spice, saffron is added to many Spanish dishes, particularly those containing rice or chicken. Avoid inexpensive saffron powders and buy saffron threads. Crush the threads just before using. A little goes a long way to give a dish a lovely golden color and a distinctive taste. Using too much saffron will give foods a medicinal taste. When used judiciously, there should be just enough to taste. To extract maximum flavor, sprinkle crushed saffron threads over a little hot water or stock and let them soak for a few minutes before adding to the dish.

paprika & chile powder

Chile pepper cultivation began in Spain soon after Columbus' voyages. Two varieties of peppers were developed — both were fully ripened, dried and ground into paprika. The milder variety adds deep color and earthy flavors, but is not hot. It makes an attractive garnish when sprinkled over deviled eggs, potato salad or other less colorful dishes. It is also used in large quantities in sauces and meat dishes.

The hotter variety is less commonly found in the U.S. It is spicy, but still milder than hot Hungarian paprika or Indian chile powder. The distinctive Spanish smoked, mild, bittersweet and hot paprikas are available at specialty grocery stores and are worth seeking out. A nice mild substitute is New Mexico chile powder, which can be used to replace mild paprika. Do not use prepared chili powder as it contains cumin, garlic and sometimes salt in addition to chile.

wine vinegar

A few drops of vinegar provide a flavor boost and balance to many dishes. Your pantry should include sherry wine vinegar, an aged red wine vinegar and a good quality white wine vinegar. Spain produces delicious mellow sherry wine vinegars with a hint of sweetness. Seek out an aged one from Jerez. Use it in salad dressings, sauces and to brighten up other dishes. Try sprinkling a few drops over roasted asparagus or a grilled steak. Store vinegar in a cool, dark place with olive oils.

olive oil

A wonderful fruity, full-flavored olive oil will make a noticeable difference in the taste of your tapas. Buy imported oil from Spain labeled "extra virgin," or substitute an Italian or California extra virgin oil. Keep the oil tightly covered and store it in a cool, dark place.

olives

Spain is the world's largest producer of green stuffed and unpitted olives. Any olive, brine-cured or oil-cured, makes wonderful tapas. Spanish black olives are seen less frequently than green olives in U.S. markets, but the more readily available Greek kalamata or French niçoise olives are delicious too. If your supermarket or deli has an olive bar, buy an assortment. Warming olives briefly in a little olive oil with spices brings out the best olive flavor.

tapas
parties & menus

Tapas are party foods! A variety of delicious and attractive dishes can be assembled to serve your friends. To make the party fun for the cook, select one or two dishes that can be made a day or two ahead, and a couple to cook on the day of the party. Then fill in with nuts, olives, cheese and bread. Tapas parties allow you to cater to your guests' tastes by serving a variety of vegetable and seafood dishes, as well as more hearty fare. Spanish-style desserts are simple. In addition to the classic Spanish flan, fruit banderillas, sliced fruit, ice cream, an orange or lemon cake, or cookies with coffee and a little brandy or sweet sherry all make a delicious finale.

Drinks, too, are easy. Chilled Spanish dry sherry, white and red wine, beer, pitchers of sangria or margaritas are all delicious with tapas. Offer a selection of beverages or serve your friends' favorite drinks.

Tapas can be served as predinner appetizers or as a complete meal. As the number of guests increases, add another dish or two. If you are running short of time, stop at the deli or market and pick up some sliced meats, marinated vegetables or salad greens to augment the menu. Buy a roasted chicken, carve it and serve with *Parsley Sauce*, page 142. Pick up some cooked shrimp and serve with *Romesco* or *Seafood Cocktail Sauce*, pages 144-145.

Tapas parties should be colorful! Use bright tablecloths and attractive serving platters. Arrange tapas and drinks on separate tables for easier circulation. Food can be served buffet-style on one table or placed on several smaller tables. Provide small bread or salad plates, forks and napkins for your guests. For easy cleanup, have a stack of small paper plates, napkins, toothpicks and plastic forks at each food area. Place several waste receptacles at strategic locations. We suggest that your guests take one or two tapas at a time and then come back for more. If tapas are being served as the main meal, have seating for everyone and use dinner plates. Set up a warming tray for the dishes that need to be served warm, or reheat for a few seconds in the microwave and pass around the hot food.

Traditional tapas parties are similar to a stand-up cocktail party, but make your guests comfortable by providing some seating and places to put down glasses and plates. For a small party of 4 to 8 people, seat them around the dining table and serve tapas buffet style.

In using the following menus, don't hesitate to reduce the number of dishes, substitute other recipes or select favorite foods to fit your group. Inviting friends to share good food, drink and conversation is one of life's great pleasures.

Mini-Tortillas, page 48

tapas
menu for six

nibbles
almonds
olives
sliced cured sausage

tapas
Deviled Eggs, page 44
Marinated Artichokes, page 54
Marinated Mushrooms, page 63
Garlic Chicken Nuggets, page 114
Oven-Roasted Baby Back Ribs,
   page 130
Warm Potato and Leek Salad,
   page 75

dessert
fresh fruit platter
cookies

preparation

❧Prepare *Wine & Garlic Chicken Nuggets, Marinated Mushrooms* and *Marinated Artichokes* 1 day before serving. Refrigerate overnight.

❧Prepare *Deviled Eggs* and *Oven-Roasted Baby Back Ribs* and refrigerate. Remove mushrooms, artichokes and eggs from refrigerator about 1 hour before serving. Make *Warm Potato and Leek Salad*. Reheat *Wine & Garlic Chicken Nuggets* and sauce, and bake *Oven-Roasted Baby Back Ribs* just before serving.

tapas
menu for six

nibbles
almonds
olives

banderillas
ham, cheese and sweet pickle chunks, small cooked shrimp, cherry tomato and roasted red pepper square, tuna chunks, cherry tomato and caperberry

tapas
Escabèche, page 92
Sherried Chicken Wings, page 116
Meatballs in Almond Sherry Sauce,
  page 126
Garbanzo Bean Salad, page 62
Stuffed Pepper Strips, page 69

dessert
sorbet and cookies

drinks
wine, sangria, beer

preparation

❧Prepare *Escabèche*, *Meatballs in Almond Sherry Sauce* and *Stuffed Pepper Strips* 1 to 2 days ahead. Start marinating *Sherried Chicken Wings*. Refrigerate.

❧Prepare *Garbanzo Bean Salad*. Bake *Sherried Chicken Wings* and remove *Escabèche* from refrigerator about 1 hour before your guests arrive. Assemble *banderillas*. Reheat meatballs and sauce.

tapas
menu for six

nibbles
almonds
olives
cubes of manchego cheese

tapas
Bagna Cauda, page 57
Beef & Potato, page 121, or
  Mushroom Empanadas, page 63
Cooked shrimp with *Romesco Sauce*,
  page 44 or *Seafood Cocktail Sauce*,
  page 145
Classic Tortilla Espanola, page 46

dessert
chilled melon slices

drinks
wine, beer, sangria

preparation

❧Bake and refrigerate *Empanadas*, *Romesco Sauce* or *Seafood Cocktail Sauce* 1 to 2 days ahead.

❧Prepare vegetables for *Bagna Cauda* and refrigerate. Cook shrimp if necessary and refrigerate. Make *Classic Tortilla Española*. About 1 hour before party, prepare *Bagna Cauda* mixture. Assemble fruit and chill.

Papas Bravas, page 74

tapas
menu for eight

nibbles
Oven-Roasted Almonds, page 26
Warm Marinated Olives, page 35

tapas
Asparagus & Ham Rolls, page 56
Fava Bean Salad Cups, page 61
Chicken, Artichoke & Oven-Dried Tomatoes,
   page 110
Scallops with Oranges and Black Olives,
   page 101
Mini-Stuffed Potatoes, page 72
Lentil & Duck Salad, page 117
Lamb Meatballs in Tomato Sauce, page 124
1 or 2 Spanish cheeses such as manchego and
   blue cabrales
baguette slices or crackers

dessert
almond, lemon or orange cake and cream
sherry.

preparation

∾One day ahead, prepare *Lentil & Duck Salad,*
Lamb Meatballs in Tomato Sauce and *Warm*
Marinated Olives. Refrigerate. Blanch and peel
the fava beans and refrigerate.

∾Cook and assemble *Asparagus & Ham Rolls,*
and *Mini-Stuffed Potatoes* in the morning and
refrigerate. Remember to remove the lentil
salad and cheese from the refrigerator at least 1
hour before serving. *Chicken, Artichoke & Oven-*
Dried Tomatoes and *Scallops with Oranges and*
Black Olives can be done just before your
guests arrive. Reheat the meatballs and bake
the potatoes just before serving. Warm the
olives. Dress the fava beans and place in lettuce
cups at the last minute.

tapas
menu for eight to ten

nibbles
almonds
olives
smoked oysters

tapas
Hot Garlic Shrimp, page 104
Marinated Cauliflower, page 58
Rainbow Peppers, page 68
Oven-Roasted Baby Potatoes with Garlic,
   page 73
Sherry Glazed Eggplant, page 60
Roasted Pork Tenderloins and *Prune and Olive
   Compote*, page 133
Chorizo-Stuffed Mushrooms, see page 122
Mini-Tortillas, page 48
Marinated Goat Cheese Rounds, page 40
French baguette slices

dessert
cookies and cream sherry

preparation

❧Prepare *Marinated Cauliflower, Rainbow Peppers, Sherry Glazed Eggplant* and *Prune and Olive Compote* for the pork and refrigerate 1 to 2 days ahead. *Mini-Tortillas* can also be baked ahead.

❧Prepare *Chorizo Stuffed Mushrooms* a few hours ahead, but bake the mushrooms and *Oven-Roasted Baby Potatoes with Garlic* at the last minute and serve warm. *Marinated Goat Cheese Rounds* can be made 1 to 2 hours ahead. Time the *Pork Tenderloins* and *Hot Garlic Shrimp*, and warm *Mini-Tortillas* so that they will be done just before your guests arrive.

tapas nibbles

The tapas tradition is based on providing a small mouthful of flavorful food to accompany a glass of wine or beer. To complement the wine and perhaps sell more, the food morsels are often salty or piquant. Small dishes of olives, nuts, potato chips or popcorn are just as welcome as more elaborate appetizers. Supermarkets and delis abound with prepackaged and prepared ingredients that can be arranged attractively on colorful plates, skewered on toothpicks or poured into bowls. For a quick party, select an assortment of cheese, ham, roast meat, pickles and olives for banderillas or canapés. Add some crackers or rounds of toasted bread, spread with a little soft cheese and top with a strip of roasted pepper or dollop of olive paste.

We've included some favorite combinations and suggestions for banderillas and canapés. Try the easy *Oven-Roasted Almonds*. They have a delicious toasted flavor and can be done ahead of time, put in an airtight jar and kept for a week. A little high-quality olive oil and gentle heating make a world of difference to the flavor and taste of *Warm Marinated Olives*. Serve easy and delicious tapas for your next gathering.

Oven-Roasted Almonds

Almonds are an essential ingredient on the tapas table. We use popcorn salt because it is more finely ground than table salt and adheres better to the nuts. This recipe doubles or triples easily.

1 cup raw, unblanched whole almonds
1 tsp. full-flavored olive oil

popcorn salt or *Seasoned Salt*, page 27

❧ Preheat oven to 275°. Place nuts in a small bowl, add olive oil and stir to coat almonds evenly. Spread almonds in a single layer in a shallow baking pan. Roast until almonds are fragrant and turn a deeper shade of brown, but are not burned, about 25 to 30 minutes. Sprinkle with salt or *Seasoned Salt*. Turn off oven and cool almonds with oven door ajar for 5 to 10 minutes. Almonds will crisp as they cool. If not used immediately, store in an airtight container.

nibbles

Seasoned Salt

Sprinkle a little of this zesty salt mixture over almonds, popcorn or eggs. If available, substitute Spanish smoked paprika for the chile powder.

2 tbs. kosher salt
1 tbs. New Mexico mild chile powder
1 tbs. ground cumin

1 tsp. hot dry mustard powder
1 tsp. ground coriander
¼ tsp. cayenne pepper, optional

❧ Blend mixture in a spice grinder, or pulverize with a mortar and pestle until very finely ground. Store in a small spice shaker or airtight jar.

nibbles

tapas
banderillas

Banderillas are 2 or 3 compatible foods served on a cocktail pick or toothpick. The name comes from the decorated barbed sticks used by banderilleros in bullfights to anger the bull before the matador comes in for the kill. Banderillas typically have streamers on the end, so using party picks with colored frills adds a nice touch. The custom is to pull off all the bite-sized morsels of food at one time and eat them all together. Banderillas are fun to eat, and they can be quickly assembled from items on the pantry shelf or in your refrigerator. Here are some suggested combinations:

- smoked oyster or mussel, piece of roasted red pepper and cherry tomato
- small piece of sardine, cheese and dill pickle slice
- chunk of solid-packed tuna, quail egg half and a piece of roasted red pepper
- pitted black olive, cheese and a piece of roasted red pepper
- marinated mushroom, sausage slice and cherry tomato
- cooked pork or beef chunk, stuffed green olive and marinated mushroom
- pickled herring, cube of cooked potato and cocktail onion or a piece of green onion
- stuffed green olive, cooked sausage slice and cube of cooked potato
- chunks of ham, cheese and sweet pickle
- cherry tomato, small cooked shrimp and caperberry without stem
- small hardboiled quail egg, rolled anchovy fillet and cherry tomato
- cube of cooked chicken, piece of marinated artichoke and cherry tomato
- cooked asparagus tip, ham and a piece of roasted pepper
- cooked shrimp, asparagus tip and cherry tomato
- cooked carrot, pitted black olive and sausage slice
- chunk of solid-packeded tuna, caperberry and a piece of roasted red pepper
- sausage slice, cheese cube and stemmed pepperoncini
- quarter of ripe fig and sausage slice or cube of ham
- cube of ripe melon wrapped in prosciutto

Sherried Chicken Liver Banderillas

Sherry wine vinegar adds a piquant taste and attractive glaze to these chicken livers.

2 to 3 chicken livers
salt and pepper to taste
2 tsp. olive oil
1 tbs. sherry wine vinegar

toothpicks
1 caperberry
1 cherry tomato or fresh fig

❧ Lightly flour chicken livers and season with salt and pepper. Heat oil in a skillet over high heat. Add chicken livers until lightly browned on all sides. Add sherry wine vinegar to skillet and cook for 1 to 2 minutes, or until livers are glazed. Cut cooked livers into bite-sized pieces, and skewer on a toothpick with a caperberry and a cherry tomato or piece of fresh fig. Serve warm.

banderillas

Fresh Fig and Prosciutto Banderillas

The sweetness of the figs complements the rich, salty flavor of the ham. Warming the figs enhances their flavor.

4 fresh ripe figs
2 tsp. lime juice
freshly ground pepper to taste

8 thin strips prosciutto
1 tsp. olive oil
toothpicks

❧ Cut figs into halves and sprinkle with lime juice and freshly ground pepper. Wrap each fig piece with a thin strip of prosciutto. Heat oil in a small skillet on high heat. Sauté fig bundles for 1 minute, or until warmed through. Skewer with toothpicks and serve warm.

banderillas

tapas
canapés

Canapés and tostas are the Spanish equivalent of Italian crostini and bruschetta. Thin slices of baguette are toasted, sometimes rubbed with garlic and topped with a flavorful ingredient or two. Assemble them just before serving so the toast stays crisp. Serve warm or at room temperature.

Leftover bread can be sliced, tightly wrapped and stored in the freezer. When you want to serve, just toast the slices without defrosting.

When you want to make canapés, heat the oven to 275° or 300° and toast bread slices until crisp and lightly browned. Spread toast with cream or goat cheese, and top with colorful and tasty roasted red or yellow peppers or tapenade. Green or black olive paste or tapenade can be found at an Italian deli or specialty food section at your local supermarket.

Here are some quick and easy **toppings**:

❧ **Goat or cream cheese** under a thin slice of ham, topped with 1 or 2 thin slices of fresh fig. Sprinkle figs with a little lime juice and generous grinds of black pepper. Serve at room temperature.

❧ **Goat or cream cheese** topped with a little tapenade, a strip of pimiento or roasted red pepper and parsley. Serve at room temperature.

❧ **Prepare** *Rainbow Peppers*, page 68, with a pinch of dried oregano, salt and pepper. Arrange a few strips over a thin layer of goat cheese. Sprinkle with parsley or cilantro. Serve at room temperature.

❧ **Layer toast** with 1 or 2 small thin slices of grilled eggplant, a few ribbons of fresh basil leaves and top with 2 or 3 *Rainbow Peppers*, page 68. Sprinkle with grated manchego or Parmesan cheese. Heat under a broiler or in a hot oven until cheese melts. Serve warm.

❧ **Cut thin slices** of ham the same size as the toasts. Place ham on the toast and top with 2 strips of roasted red pepper and a thin slice of manchego or Gruyère cheese. Run under a broiler just until cheese melts. Serve warm.

❧ **Cut thin slices** of ham the same size as the toasts. Place ham on the toast, spread with a thin layer of Dijon mustard and top with 1 or 2 small cooked asparagus spears and a thin slice of manchego or fontina cheese. Heat under a broiler or in a hot oven until cheese melts. Serve warm.

❧ **Pulse cubes** of leftover roast pork or beef in a food processor. Add a few pimiento-stuffed olives or capers, prepared mustard and mayonnaise. Pulse until meat is coarsely chopped and mixture holds together. Spread on toast and garnish with 1 or 2 slices of stuffed olives or 1 to 2 capers. Serve at room temperature.

❧ **Spread toasts** with a thin layer of *Aïoli*, page 140, and top with a thin tomato slice and 2 or 3 small cooked shrimp. Season with salt and pepper. Garnish with a few ribbons of fresh basil leaves. Serve at room temperature.

❧ **Spread toasts** with a thin layer of *Aïoli*, page 140, and top with thin slices of cooked marinated artichoke hearts and 1 or 2 strips of roasted red peppers. Sprinkle tops with grated manchego or Parmesan cheese. Heat in a hot oven until just warmed through.

Fresh Pear and Anchovy Toasts

Choose a perfectly ripe pear and use good quality oil-packed anchovies. Prepare toasts just before serving so they stay crisp and pears do not turn brown.

10 to 12 baguette slices, about ½-inch thick
2 to 3 tsp. full-flavored olive oil
1 clove garlic, peeled

1 ripe Comice, Bartlett or Peckham pear
2 tbs. lemon juice
freshly ground black pepper
10 to 12 anchovy fillets

❧ Preheat oven to 350°. Place bread slices on a baking sheet. Brush each slice with a little olive oil. Bake until lightly browned and crisp, about 10 to 12 minutes. Cut garlic in half and rub the top of each toasted slice with the cut surface of garlic clove. Peel and core pear, quarter and cut each quarter into 5 thin slices. Pour lemon juice into a shallow pan, add pear slices and gently toss to coat. Grind fresh black pepper over pear slices. Rinse anchovies with water, drain and pat dry with paper towels. To assemble, place 1 or 2 pear slices on each garlic-rubbed toast and top with a strip of anchovy.

canapés

Warm Marinated Olives

Warmed marinated olives are very enticing. Combine 2 or 3 different kinds and colors of unpitted olives such as kalamata, manzanilla and other favorites. Imported black olives have more character than domestic ones.

1 cup assorted unpitted olives
2 tbs. full-flavored olive oil
¼ tsp. cumin seeds, lightly cracked
¼ tsp. anise seeds, lightly cracked
1 bay leaf
6 to 8 black peppercorns

2 cloves garlic, thinly sliced
8 to 10 caperberries, optional
3 to 4 drops red or green Tabasco Sauce
1 tbs. coarsely grated orange zest

Rinse olives under cold water and pat dry. With the tip of a sharp knife, cut 2 or 3 small slits through to the pit in each olive. Heat oil in a saucepan over low heat. Add cumin, anise seeds, bay leaf, peppercorns and garlic. Sauté garlic for 3 to 4 minutes, or until soft. Add caperberries, Tabasco, orange zest and olives. Stir briefly, remove from heat and cool to room temperature. Cover tightly and refrigerate for several hours or overnight. Just before serving, heat olive mixture in a small saucepan over low heat. Cook until warm to the touch. Remove bay leaf; pour into a serving bowl and serve immediately.

canapés

cheese & egg *tapas*

If you have some cheese and eggs in the refrigerator, it is easy to put together some savory tapas. A few cubes of cheese alone serve as tasty tapas, and with some ham or prosciutto slices, a few olives and a glass of wine, your guests will be content. Don't hesitate to substitute one of your favorites in these recipes. Quesadillas can also be assembled quickly from other tapas ingredients. Deviled eggs are easily dressed up with capers or olives and make great party fare. The Spanish are known for their classic potato and egg tortilla. Included are recipes for the *Classic Tortilla Espanola* and *Mini-Tortillas*. Serve them as tapas or take them on a picnic. They can be made ahead of time and reheated in the microwave for breakfast or a company brunch.

Marinated Goat Cheese Rounds, page 40

Apple, Walnut & Blue Cheese Balls

These can be made an hour or two ahead and refrigerated until ready to serve. Arrange the cheese balls on a bed of lettuce leaves or some watercress and accompany with crackers. Serve with red wine.

4 oz. blue cheese, crumbled
⅓ cup chopped toasted walnuts
1 Gala or Golden Delicious apple,
    about 7 oz.

2 tsp. lemon juice
½ cup finely chopped parsley
crackers

In a small bowl, combine crumbled blue cheese and walnuts. Set aside. Peel and core apple, and grate coarsely in a food processor or with a grater. Place in a small bowl, add lemon juice and toss to combine. Add walnuts and cheese mixture to apples and mix well. Form into 1-inch balls. Roll in parsley and arrange on a serving platter.

cheese & egg

Hot Goat Cheese Toasts

•MAKES ABOUT 20 PIECES

Small toasts are topped with a savory, fresh goat cheese mixture and heated under the broiler. Serve immediatley.

5 oz. fresh mild goat cheese
½ tsp. fresh thyme leaves
1 tbs. coarsely chopped capers, drained
1 tbs. finely chopped sun-dried tomatoes,
　oil-packed and drained

⅛ tsp. mild New Mexico chile powder
generous grinds of black pepper
20 (2- to 3-inch) toast rounds

❧ Preheat broiler. Position oven rack about 6 inches below heat source. Line a cookie sheet with aluminum foil. In a small bowl, combine goat cheese, thyme, capers, sun-dried tomatoes, chile powder and pepper and mix well. Spread each toast round with about 2 teaspoons of goat cheese. Place under broiler and heat until cheese is hot and slightly puffy, about 2 minutes. Watch carefully as these brown quickly. Remove toasts and place on a serving plate.

❧ To make toasts: Preheat oven to 300°. Slice a day-old baguette, 2 to 3 inches in diameter, and cut into ¼-inch slices. Place on cookie sheet and toast until lightly browned, about 15 minutes. Turn slices over and bake until crisp, about another 10 minutes. Store in an airtight container until ready to serve.

cheese & egg

Marinated Goat Cheese Rounds

Tangy fresh goat cheese is complemented with a little full-flavored olive oil, garlic and spice. Make this an hour or two ahead, cover and keep at cool room temperature until ready to serve. Accompany with a small basket of baguette slices or crackers.

8 oz. fresh goat cheese log
5 slices *Rainbow Peppers*, page 68, or roasted red pepper or pimiento pieces
10 black olives, pitted and halved or quartered

3 tbs. full-flavored olive oil
pinch dried red pepper flakes
4 cloves garlic, thinly sliced
¼ tsp. ground cumin
2 tsp. lemon juice
generous grinds black pepper

❧ Cut cheese log into ½-inch rounds. Arrange cheese rounds on a serving plate. Place a strip of pepper on each slice and scatter olive pieces over cheese. Heat olive oil in a saucepan over low heat. Add pepper flakes and garlic slices. Cook and stir for about 2 to 3 minutes, or until garlic softens and is lightly browned. Add cumin and remove from heat. Cool to room temperature. Pour olive oil over cheese slices and sprinkle with a little lemon juice. Grind some black pepper over each round and dust paprika over top. Serve at room temperature.

cheese & egg

Baked Olive Balls

Pimiento-stuffed olives or cubes of melted cheese form the centers for these satisfying tapas.

1 ¼ cups all-purpose flour
½ tsp. baking powder
¼ tsp. salt
1 tsp. paprika
½ tsp. ground cumin
pinch cayenne pepper, optional
¼ cup grated Parmesan or pecorino
   cheese

¼ cup olive oil
1 large egg
2 to 3 tbs. ice water
25 small Spanish olives stuffed with
   pimiento

Preheat oven to 350°. Line a large cookie sheet with parchment paper. Place flour, baking powder, salt, paprika, cumin, cayenne and Parmesan cheese in a food processor and pulse 2 to 3 times until well mixed. Add olive oil, egg and ice water. Process until dough comes together. Dry olives with paper towels. Flatten a scant 2 teaspoons of the dough with your fingers into a 2-inch diameter disk. Place olive in middle and enclose in the dough. Roll between your palms to seal the seams and make a uniformly smooth ball. Place on a cookie sheet. Bake until lightly browned, about 20 minutes. Serve warm. If made ahead, these can be reheated in the oven for 5 minutes.

Variation: Fill balls with ½-inch cubes of sharp cheddar or hot pepper Jack cheese.

cheese & egg

Marinated Manchego Cheese

Manchego cheese takes on a nutty character after a few days of marinating in olive oil. Use the best quality oil available. Add a few dried red chile flakes and some crushed thyme or rosemary leaves to flavor the oil for an interesting variation.

½ lb. aged manchego cheese
⅓ cup full-flavored olive oil

dried red pepper flakes, thyme or rosemary, optional

❧ Remove rind from cheese and discard. Cut cheese into triangles about 1 inch on a side and ⅛-inch thick. Place cheese in a small container and add enough oil to cover cheese. Sprinkle with red pepper flakes or herbs, if using. Cover cheese with a tight-fitting lid. Refrigerate and shake container occasionally for 4 to 5 days. Marinated cheese can be kept in the refrigerator for 1 month. Serve at room temperature.

❧ Place cheese and some of the oil into a shallow serving bowl. Provide a small fork or toothpicks to spear the cheese, and accompany with small pieces of bread or plain water crackers.

cheese & egg

Grilled Swiss Chard & Cheese Packages

Blanched Swiss chard leaves are wrapped around a piece of firm cheese topped with a little tapenade or slivers of sun-dried tomatoes. Assemble ahead of time and grill when ready to serve. These are best served warm.

8 cups water
10 Swiss chard leaves
6 oz. manchego, Gruyère or Gouda
   cheese

2 tbs. tapenade or olive paste
olive oil

❧ Bring water to a boil in a large saucepan. Wash chard and blanch in boiling water for 30 seconds, or until softened. Remove from water and drain on paper towels. With a sharp knife, cut out the tough stem. Cut large leaves in half horizontally and trim to make 3½- to 4-inch squares. Overlap leaves where the stem was removed. Cut cheese into 1½-inch squares, about ¼-inch thick. Place one piece of cheese in center of each leaf and top cheese with about 1 teaspoon of tapenade. Fold in sides of leaf to make a compact package. Lightly brush both sides of package with olive oil. When ready to serve, grill for about 1 minute on each side, or until cheese feels soft to the touch through the leaf.

Filling Variations

• Replace tapenade with 5 to 6 sun-dried tomatoes, oil-packed. Cut tomatoes into slivers.

• Cut full-flavored, thin-sliced ham into 1½-inch pieces, spread lightly with mustard and top with cheese.

• Place a ¼-inch slice of spicy cooked sausage on top of the cheese.

cheese & egg

Deviled Eggs with Olives

· MAKES 8 PIECES

Use pimiento-stuffed Spanish olives, imported black olives or some of each. Refrigerate eggs until ready to serve.

4 hard-boiled eggs
1 tbs. mayonnaise
1 tbs. Dijon mustard
4 to 5 large olives, chopped

salt and freshly ground pepper
1 tbs. finely chopped parsley or cilantro for garnish

❧ Cut cooked eggs in half. Carefully remove yolks and place in a small bowl. Mash yolks with a fork. Add mayonnaise, mustard, chopped olives, salt and pepper and mix well. Divide filling among cooked egg white halves. Sprinkle with parsley or cilantro for garnish.

cheese & egg

Deviled Eggs with Capers

Stuffed hard-boiled eggs are popular Spanish tapas. Double or triple this recipe depending on the size of your party. Refrigerate until ready to serve.

4 hard-boiled eggs
1 tbs. mayonnaise
½ tsp. anchovy paste
1 tbs. Dijon mustard
1 tbs. coarsely chopped capers, rinsed
   and drained

salt and freshly ground pepper
paprika for garnish
16 to 20 whole capers

❧ Cut cooked eggs in half. Carefully remove yolks and place in a small bowl. Mash yolks with a fork. Add mayonnaise, anchovy, mustard, capers, salt and pepper and mix well. Divide filling among cooked egg white halves. Sprinkle with paprika and garnish each egg with 2 or 3 whole capers.

cheese & egg

Classic Tortilla Española

This delicious potato omelet is found in all regions of Spain. Be sure to save the drained oil from the cooked potatoes — it has a wonderful flavor and can be used to sauté vegetables or seafood.

½ cup full-flavored olive oil
1 clove garlic, peeled and halved
1 medium onion, halved and thinly
　sliced
1½ lb. boiling potatoes, peeled and cut
　into ⅛-inch slices

6 large eggs
salt and freshly ground white pepper
Tabasco Sauce, optional

❧ Heat oil in a 9- or 10-inch nonstick skillet over medium heat. Add garlic and cook until lightly browned. Remove and discard garlic. Add onion slices and simmer in oil for 2 to 3 minutes. Slide potato slices into oil a few at a time to keep them from sticking together. Cover pan and simmer potatoes over medium heat for 25 to 30 minutes. Gently move potatoes around several times during cooking. Test with a fork for doneness. When potatoes are cooked through, but not browned, pour them into a large strainer over a heatproof bowl to catch the oil. Drain for several minutes and reserve oil.

❧ Break eggs into a large bowl. Season well with salt and pepper. Add a few drops of Tabasco Sauce if desired. Whisk together eggs. Spoon in the potato-onion mixture and gently combine, keeping potato slices as whole as possible. Wipe out skillet with a paper towel and place over medium heat. Add 2 tablespoons of the reserved oil and heat until hot. Pour in the egg-potato mixture and reduce heat to medium. Shake the pan frequently to keep the eggs from sticking to the pan. When the eggs have set on the sides of the pan and have

cheese & egg

started to brown, place a flat lid or plate over the pan. Over the sink or an easily cleanable surface, deftly invert the pan onto the lid or plate and then slide the tortilla back into the pan to cook the other side. A perfectly cooked tortilla is barely set in the center, with a lightly browned surface on both sides.

❧ Turn out onto a serving plate and cool before serving. Cut into wedges or squares. Serve warm or at room temperature.

Variation: Add a favorite vegetable or cooked meat to the potato mixture. We'd suggest trying diced green chiles, diced ham, chopped well-drained, squeezed-dry spinach, flaked tuna, green peas or crumbled cooked sausage.

Classic Tortilla Española

Mini-Tortillas

• Makes 12 individual tortillas

This version of the classic Spanish potato and egg dish is baked in a muffin pan. The individual small tortillas are easy to serve and can be prepared ahead of time. Leftovers can be tucked into a lunch box.

1 tbs. full-flavored olive oil
1 medium onion, diced, about 1 cup
2 cloves garlic, minced
2 cups diced cooked potatoes, in ¼-inch dice

7 large eggs
½ tsp. salt
¼ tsp. ground white pepper
½ cup diced pimiento or roasted green chiles

❧ Heat olive oil in a medium skillet over medium heat. Add onion and reduce heat to low. Cook and cover onions until tender and translucent, but not browned, about 5 minutes. Add garlic and cook an additional 1 to 2 minutes. Add cooked potatoes and toss to coat with onion and oil mixture. Remove pan from heat and cool for a few minutes.

❧ Preheat oven to 350°. In a large bowl, whisk together eggs until well combined. Add salt, pepper and pimiento. Add cooled potato-onion mixture and any remaining olive oil to eggs. Gently stir to combine. Use a 12-cup nonstick muffin pan with 3-inch diameter muffin cups. Lightly oil each muffin cup. Fill muffin cups evenly with potato egg mixture. Bake until tortillas are lightly browned on the top and just set in the center, about 18 to 20 minutes. Remove tortillas from pan while hot and place on a serving platter. Serve warm or at room temperature.

❧ These can be baked ahead of time, and will keep for a day or two in the refrigerator. Reheat for a few minutes in an oven, or warm slightly in the microwave for a few seconds.

cheese & egg

Portobello Mushroom & Goat Cheese Quesadillas

Mexican-style tortillas stuffed with a flavorful filling, while not Spanish, make satisfying tapas. Quesadillas can be made in a skillet, but it is easier to bake several at one time in the oven.

4 flour tortillas, about 7- to 8-inch rounds
olive oil
1 cup *Sautéed Portobello Mushrooms*, page 65
⅓ cup diced roasted red peppers or pimientos

1 to 2 tbs. capers, rinsed and patted dry
1 cup crumbled fresh goat cheese
⅓ cup grated Parmesan or pecorino cheese
dried red pepper flakes

❧ Preheat oven to 450°. Line a baking sheet with foil. To assemble, brush one side of each flour tortilla with a little olive oil. Place two tortillas oiled side down on a baking sheet. Arrange mushrooms, peppers and capers over tortillas. Top with goat and Parmesan cheese. Sprinkle with red pepper flakes and top with remaining flour tortillas, placing the oiled side up. Bake until lightly browned, about 8 to 10 minutes. Cut each into 8 wedges and serve immediately.

❧ To cook in a skillet, place each assembled quesadilla in a nonstick skillet. Heat over medium heat for 3 to 4 minutes, or until bottom tortilla is lightly browned. Using a large spatula, turn the quesadilla over to brown the other side. Cook for 2 to 3 minutes, or until cheese melts and bottom tortilla is lightly browned. Slide each quesadilla onto a cutting board and cut into 8 wedges. Serve hot.

cheese & egg

Chicken & Rainbow Peppers Quesadillas

Use thin slices of leftover roasted chicken or pork in this appetizing quesadilla.

4 flour tortillas, about 7- to 8-inch round
olive oil
⅓ cup *Romesco Sauce*, page 144
¾ cup grated mozzarella or manchego
  cheese
4 to 6 slices chicken, cut into 2-inch
  pieces

½ cup *Rainbow Peppers*, page 68,
  cut into 2-inch pieces
¼ cup grated pecorino or Parmesan
  cheese

❧ Preheat oven to 450°. Line a baking sheet with foil. Brush one side of each flour tortilla with a little olive oil and place 2 tortillas oiled side down on a baking sheet. Spread each with *Romesco Sauce* and sprinkle with cheese. Distribute chicken slices and peppers over cheese and sprinkle with Parmesan cheese. Top with a second tortilla, oiled side up. Bake until lightly browned, about 8 to 10 minutes. Place each quesadilla on a cutting board and cut each into 8 wedges. Serve immediately.

❧ To cook in a skillet, place each assembled quesadilla in a nonstick skillet. Heat over medium heat for 3 to 4 minutes, or until bottom tortilla is lightly browned. Using a large spatula, turn the quesadilla over to brown the other side. Cook 2 to 3 minutes, or until cheese melts and bottom tortilla is lightly browned. Slide each quesadilla out onto a cutting board and cut into 8 wedges. Serve hot.

cheese & egg

Quesadilla ideas

❧ Combine thin slices of *Roasted Pork Tenderloins*, page 132, and *Prune and Olive Compote*, page 133, with grated manchego cheese and some dried red pepper flakes.

❧ Fill tortillas with homemade chorizo from *Chorizo-Stuffed Mushroom Caps*, page 122, *Oven-Dried Tomatoes*, page 79, and grated mozzarella and Parmesan cheese.

❧ Make a quesadilla with 2 or 3 different kinds of grated cheese and spoon a little *Parsley Sauce*, page 142, over cheese.

❧ Layer thin slices of roasted chicken or pork over grated mozzarella and top with small spoonfuls of *Olive Pâté*, page 66. Peel, seed and chop tomatoes and drain liquid.

❧ Layer fresh goat cheese, *Rainbow Peppers*, page 68, or pimiento strips and dot with prepared tapenade or olive paste.

❧ Sprinkle grated Monterey Jack cheese with cooked small shrimp, diced green chiles and chopped fresh cilantro.

cheese & egg

tapas
vegetable-based

Vegetables contribute a sparkle, texture and lightness to the tapas table. Gorgeous red and yellow roasted peppers, crisp bright green asparagus and fava beans, flavorful tomatoes, potatoes and garlic all serve to complement heartier meat-based tapas. Versatile vegetables adapt well to roasting, grilling, broiling and baking. Vegetables are terrific served alone or when used to top pizzettes, or use as a filling for empanadas or combine in savory salads. If there is only time to make one vegetable dish, be sure to make *Rainbow Peppers* or *Stuffed Pepper Strips*.

Asparagus & Ham Rolls, Page 56

tapas
vegetable-based

Another traditional tapas vegetable is the potato. You will find several tempting recipes including *Mini-Stuffed Potatoes*, which can be cooked, stuffed ahead of time and baked just before serving. *Spicy Baked Potato Wedges* accompanied with a spicy tomato sauce and *Oven-Roasted Baby Potatoes with Garlic* are easy oven dishes.

Bagna Cauda with a variety of fresh or lightly cooked vegetables dipped into a warm garlicky sauce is a perfect focal point of a tapas party. This dish also goes nicely with grilled chicken or steaks as the featured main course. Include some of these flavorful vegetable dishes on your tapas table.

Mini-Stuffed Potatoes, page 72

Marinated Artichokes

Artichokes are a favorite tapas item. In this recipe the artichokes are cut into quarters with an inch or two of tender stem left attached. Prepare this dish a day ahead so flavors have time to blend.

2 lemons, divided
4 medium-sized artichokes, about
   3-inch diameter
½ cup white wine vinegar
¼ cup full-flavored olive oil

2 cloves garlic, chopped
⅛ tsp. red pepper flakes
10 to 12 mint leaves, finely chopped
salt and freshly ground black pepper

✎ Juice lemons. Reserve 2 tablespoons of juice for cooking artichokes. Combine remaining juice, lemon halves and 4 to 5 cups of water in a large bowl. Using a sharp knife, cut 1-inch off the top of each artichoke and discard. Cut the stem, leaving a ¾- to 1-inch stem at bottom. Remove 3 to 4 layers of tough outside leaves until you reach tender light green leaves underneath. Cut each artichoke into quarters. Using a small sharp knife or potato peeler, peel stem and evenly trim area where leaves were removed. Cut out any sharp or prickly areas in the center of the artichoke. Immediately submerge trimmed artichokes in a bowl with lemons and water. Bring 3 cups of water to a boil in a 3-quart saucepan. Add reserved lemon juice and wine vinegar. Remove artichokes from acidulated water and place in a saucepan. Reduce heat and gently boil uncovered for 15 to 20 minutes. Stir occasionally. Start checking doneness at 15 minutes, piercing artichoke bottom with a knife blade. When artichokes are tender, carefully remove them to a strainer and drain for a few minutes.

vegetables

Heat oil in a small skillet over medium heat. Add garlic and red pepper flakes. Cook for 2 to 3 minutes, or until garlic softens. Place drained artichokes in a bowl, pour over garlic and oil, and add mint, salt and pepper. Toss gently to combine. Cover and refrigerate until 30 minutes before serving. Serve on small plates with forks.

Marinated Artichokes

Asparagus & Ham Rolls

*Asparagus spears are wrapped in a mustard-glazed ham slice, about 3- by 4- inches in size. Tuck in a strip of **Rainbow Peppers**, page 68, for a colorful and delicious variation. Serve at a cool room temperature.*

1 lb. large cooked asparagus spears
½ lb. thin Black Forest or boiled ham slices

2 tbs. Dijon mustard
1 tbs. sour cream or heavy cream
freshly ground pepper

❧ Trim asparagus spears so they are slightly longer than ham pieces. Combine mustard with sour cream. Season with pepper. With a pastry brush or knife, lightly spread a little mustard mixture on one side of ham slices. Place asparagus on ham with asparagus tip slightly above top of ham slice. Roll so that asparagus tip shows. Arrange on a serving plate.

Variation: If you have some *Rainbow Peppers* on hand, include a pepper strip with the asparagus spear.

Note: To make more servings or if using thin asparagus, use 2 spears per roll. Position one spear with the tip showing at the top of the ham slice and one tip showing at the bottom of the slice. Roll up and cut rolls in half.

vegetables

Bagna Cauda

This dish originated in Italy, but it incorporates basic Spanish flavors of garlic, anchovy and olive oil. It means "hot bath" and makes a zesty dip for raw, cooked or grilled vegetables.

1 can (2 oz.) flat anchovy fillets
½ cup full-flavored olive oil
½ cup butter
6 cloves garlic, finely chopped

½ tsp. salt
⅛ tsp. dried red pepper flakes
raw and cooked vegetables
1½-inch French bread cubes

❧ Drain oil from anchovies into a small saucepan. Finely chop anchovies. Add anchovies, butter and oil and heat over low heat. Stir until butter melts. Add garlic, salt and red pepper flakes. Cook gently, stirring occasionally, for 10 minutes, or until garlic is soft but not browned and anchovies have dissolved. Pour sauce into a small serving bowl and keep warm on a warming tray, set over a candle or use a fondue pot. Stir sauce occasionally to redistribute garlic from the bottom. Arrange raw and cooked vegetables and cubed bread on a platter with a container of skewers nearby. Spear vegetables on wood skewers or fondue forks and dip into warm oil. Use a cube of bread to catch any drops of oil from the vegetables.

❧ Use the following raw vegetables for dipping: red, green or yellow pepper strips, carrot slices or strips, fennel or celery strips, zucchini or yellow squash slices, small mushroom caps or cherry tomatoes.

❧ Use the following as cooked vegetables: blanch asparagus, snow peas, broccoli or cauliflower florets for 1 minute in boiling water or microwave briefly. Small cooked creamer potatoes, celery root cubes, parsnip slices or grilled baby leeks are delicious dippers as well.

vegetables

Marinated Cauliflower

• Makes 4 to 6 servings

Steamed cauli-flower florets are lightly dressed with a lemon and olive oil vinaigrette. This can be done a day ahead and refrigerated. Remove from the refrigerator about 30 minutes before serving. Serve with toothpicks.

1 large head cauliflower, cut into florets
2 tbs. lemon juice
2 tbs. full-flavored olive oil

salt and freshly ground pepper
pimiento pieces and a few black olives
 for garnish

❧ Steam cauliflower florets over boiling water for 3 to 4 minutes, or until crisp-tender. Remove from heat and pour into a shallow serving bowl. Whisk together lemon juice, olive oil, salt and pepper, and pour over hot florets. Gently toss to combine florets with dressing. Garnish with pimientos and olives. Serve at room temperature.

vegetables

Eggplant & Tomato Tartlets

Eggplant and garlic are roasted together in the oven to make a flavorful filling for small pastry shells.

1 medium eggplant, about 1 lb.
2 tsp. olive oil
salt and freshly ground pepper
1 bulb garlic, unpeeled
½ cup *Oven-Dried Tomatoes*,
   page 79, or ¼ cup sun-dried
   tomatoes, oil-packed

½ tsp. chopped fresh thyme leaves
1 tbs. chopped fresh mint leaves
2 tbs. crumbled blue or goat cheese
16 tartlets from *Basic Tartlet Pastry*,
   page 152, baked and cooled

❧ Preheat oven to 350°. Cut eggplant in half lengthwise, and with a sharp knife make several diagonal cuts about ½-inch deep in flesh. Drizzle with olive oil and season with salt and pepper. Line a cookie sheet with foil and place eggplant on foil, cut sides up. Cut off about ½ inch from the top of the garlic bulb, slicing off the tips of the individual cloves. Place on a small sheet of aluminum foil and drizzle with olive oil. Wrap garlic tightly in foil and place on a cookie sheet with eggplant. Bake eggplant and garlic until tender, about 35 to 40 minutes.

❧ When eggplant is cool, scoop flesh from shells and place in a strainer. Allow to drain for 10 minutes and place in a medium bowl. Squeeze pulp from 4 or 5 roasted garlic cloves, chop or mash with a fork until smooth, and add to eggplant. Chop tomatoes into ½-inch pieces. Add tomatoes, thyme and mint leaves to the eggplant. Stir in cheese and season with salt and pepper. Fill pastry shells with about 1 tablespoon of filling just before serving.

vegetables

Sherry-Glazed Eggplant

• MAKES 4 TO 6 SERVINGS

Eggplant cubes braised in an aromatic sherry and garlic sauce make quick and easy tapas. Use long slender Asian eggplants since they retain their shape and have an excellent flavor.

1 lb. Asian eggplants, 1- to 2-inch diameter, about 4 or 5
2 tbs. olive oil
½ cup finely chopped onion
2 large cloves garlic, finely chopped
1 tsp. paprika

⅔ cup chicken broth
⅓ cup cream sherry
1 tbs. sherry wine vinegar
1 tbs. tomato paste
salt and freshly ground pepper
2 tbs. chopped fresh cilantro for garnish

❧ Trim eggplant; cut in half lengthwise and then cut each half into ¾-inch slices. Heat oil over high heat in a large sauté pan until it is almost smoking. Add eggplant and stir, about 2 to 3 minutes. Add onion, garlic and paprika to skillet and cook for another minute. Add chicken broth, sherry, wine vinegar and tomato paste. Season with salt and pepper and mix well. Reduce heat to low, cover and braise for 10 minutes, or until eggplant is tender and the sauce has thickened slightly, stirring once or twice. Remove from heat. Garnish with cilantro just before serving. Serve warm or at room temperature with toothpicks.

vegetables

Fava Bean Salad Cups

Fresh fava beans are one of the first harbingers of spring and have a delightful taste. It takes a little labor to peel them, but their special flavor pairs well with ham or prosciutto and cheese. You can substitute baby green lima beans for the favas.

1 ½ lb. fava beans in the pod
¼ cup diced ham, cut into ¼-inch dice
¼ cup coarsely grated manchego or
    Parmesan cheese
4 to 5 fresh mint leaves, finely chopped
1 tbs. full-flavored olive oil
1 tsp. Dijon mustard

1 tsp. red wine vinegar
salt and freshly ground pepper
12 to 14 nicely shaped small
    butter lettuce leaves or romaine
    lettuce leaves
fresh mint leaves for garnish

❧ Remove fava beans from large outer pod. Blanch favas in boiling water for 1 minute and drain. When cool enough to handle, remove the thick skin from each bean and discard. There will be about ⅔ cup of peeled fava beans. Combine peeled fava beans, ham, cheese and mint leaves. In a separate small bowl, whisk together olive oil, mustard, red wine vinegar, salt and pepper. Toss fava beans with dressing and adjust seasoning. Spoon a little of the bean mixture into small lettuce leaves and arrange on a platter. Garnish cups with a few mint leaves. Serve at room temperature.

vegetables

Garbanzo Bean Salad

Garbanzo beans were brought to Spain by the Moors and remain very popular today. Canned garbanzo beans are readily available and work perfectly in this hearty salad.

1 can (15 oz.) garbanzo beans, drained
1 cup peeled, seeded and chopped
  tomatoes
4 to 5 green onions, white part only,
  thinly sliced

½ cup diced ham pieces, optional
½ tsp. dried oregano
2 tbs. full-flavored olive oil
1 tbs. plus 1 tsp. sherry wine vinegar
salt and freshly ground pepper

Rinse drained garbanzo beans with cold water and drain well. Pat dry and place in a serving bowl. Add tomatoes, onions, ham and oregano and mix well. Whisk together olive oil, vinegar, salt and pepper in a small bowl. Pour over beans and toss gently to coat with dressing. Serve on small plates at room temperature.

Variation: Substitute small chunks of sausage, cooked chicken, roasted red peppers or artichoke hearts for the ham.

vegetables

Marinated Mushrooms

Small white-button mushrooms about 1-inch diameter are perfect for tapas. If small mushrooms aren't available, use larger ones and cut into halves or quarters.

½ lb. small mushrooms
2 tbs. olive oil
2 cloves garlic, finely sliced
2 tbs. sherry wine vinegar
2 tbs. water
½ tsp. dried tarragon

½ tsp. brown sugar
dash Tabasco Sauce
salt and freshly ground pepper
freshly chopped parsley or small pieces
   of pimiento for garnish

❧ Cut off mushroom stems flush with mushroom caps. Clean mushroom caps and set aside. Heat oil in a small saucepan over low heat. Add garlic and cook for 1 to 2 minutes, or until softened. Add mushrooms and stir to coat with oil. Continue to cook for 1 to 2 minutes. Add vinegar, water, tarragon, sugar, Tabasco, salt and pepper. Cover pan and simmer over low heat for 5 minutes, stirring once or twice. Cool mushrooms in marinade. These can be refrigerated for 3 to 4 days. To serve, lift from marinade, place in a serving bowl and garnish with parsley or pimiento. Serve at room temperature with toothpicks.

vegetables

Mushroom Empanadas

Small savory mushroom empanadas are popular tapas. Make the filling first so it has time to cool before assembling empanadas. Use the more flavorful brown cremino mushrooms.

1 tbs. full-flavored olive oil
¼ cup finely chopped large shallots, about 4
1 lb. brown or white mushrooms, finely chopped
salt and freshly ground pepper
½ cup grated Monterey Jack or Gruyère cheese
¼ cup finely diced flavorful ham, optional
1 tsp. dried tarragon
2 tsp. lemon juice
a few drops Tabasco Sauce
Basic Empanada Pastry, page 148
1 egg white

❧ Heat oil in a medium skillet over medium-low heat. Add shallots and cook for 1 to 2 minutes, or until soft. Increase heat; add mushrooms, salt and pepper. Cook for 3 to 4 minutes, stirring, or until mushroom juice is released and the mixture is quite dry. Remove from heat and cool for 15 minutes. Stir in cheese, ham, tarragon, lemon juice and Tabasco. Glaze with egg white.

❧ Assemble and bake empandas as instructed in *Basic Empanada Pastry*, see page 148.

Baked empanadas can be frozen. Preheat oven to 350°. Place frozen empanadas on a cookie sheet and bake until hot, about 15 to 20 minutes. If empanadas have been refrigerated, reheat until warm to the touch, about 7 to 10 minutes.

vegetables

Sautéed Portobello Mushrooms

*Meaty and flavor-ful portobello mushroom strips make a wonderful topping for **Pizzettes**, page 80, or **Portobello Mushroom & Goat Cheese Quesadilla**, page 49; or serve with **Wine & Garlic Chicken Nuggets**, page 114.*

2 medium portobello mushrooms, about 4 oz. each
1 tbs. olive oil
1 clove garlic, mined

salt and freshly ground pepper
½ cup chicken broth
2 tsp. lemon juice
chopped parsley for garnish

❧ Remove stems from mushrooms and discard. Use a sharp spoon to gently scrape out black gills and discard. Cut mushrooms into ⅛-inch strips. Heat oil and garlic in a skillet over medium heat. Add garlic and sauté for about 1 to 2 minutes, or until softened but do not brown. Add mushrooms and toss for 2 to 3 minutes or until mushrooms are soft. Season with salt and a generous amount of black pepper. Add chicken broth and continue cooking mushrooms over high heat until liquid has almost evaporated. Remove from heat, sprinkle with lemon juice and serve warm or at room temperature. Garnish with parsley.

vegetables

Olive Pâté

Spread this colorful pâté on crackers or jícama slices or use it to stuff cherry tomatoes. This will keep for several days in the refrigerator.

1 cup pimiento-stuffed green olives, drained, about 6 oz.
1 hard-boiled egg, chopped
1 to 2 green onions, white part only, finely chopped
1 tbs. capers, drained and rinsed
½ tsp. dried marjoram
freshly ground pepper
1½ tbs. mayonnaise
1 tbs. whipped cream cheese
1 tbs. cream sherry

 Rinse olives under cold water and dry on paper towels. Add olives, egg, onions and capers in a food processor. Pulse 5 to 6 times until mixture is coarsely chopped, about the size of small peas. Spoon into a small bowl, and add marjoram, pepper, mayonnaise, cheese and sherry. Combine well. Refrigerate until ready to serve.

vegetables

Sweet & Sour Pearl Onions

Frozen pearl onions work beautifully in this dish and don't need any peeling. Serve warm or at room temperature with toothpicks.

1 tbs. full-flavored olive oil
1 pkg. (10 oz.) frozen petite whole
   onions
2 tbs. water

2 tsp. brown sugar
¼ cup apple cider vinegar
salt and freshly ground pepper

Heat oil in a medium skillet over medium-low heat. Add onions and water. Cover, lower heat and simmer for 10 minutes, shaking the pan occasionally. Add sugar, vinegar, salt and pepper. Uncover, increase heat to medium-high and continue to cook for 5 minutes, or until onions are tender and liquid has evaporated. Shake pan frequently. Pour into a small serving bowl.

vegetables

Rainbow Peppers

• MAKES 4 TO 6 SERVINGS

A combination of red, yellow, orange or green bell peppers make attractive and easy tapas. Keep some of these on hand in your refrigerator. Serve in a shallow bowl or with a soft cheese on toasted bread. Also try a few strips on a sandwich or in a salad.

1 large red bell pepper
1 large yellow bell pepper
1 large orange or green bell pepper
2 tbs. olive oil

salt and freshly ground pepper
2 cloves garlic, thinly sliced
⅓ cup water
2 tbs. sherry wine vinegar

Cut peppers in half, remove stem and ribs and cut into ½-inch strips. If peppers are quite long, cut the strips in half. Heat oil in a large skillet over medium-high heat. Add pepper strips and sauté for 2 to 3 minutes. Season with salt and pepper. Add garlic slices and toss to coat with oil. Pour in water and vinegar. Reduce heat to low, and simmer covered for 20 to 25 minutes, or until peppers are soft. Uncover and cook over high heat for 2 to 3 minutes, or until liquid has reduced to a syrup. Serve at room temperature.

vegetables

Stuffed Pepper Strips

• Makes about 4 to 6 pieces

Red or yellow bell peppers are baked with a savory garlic and breadcrumb topping. Serve warm or at room temperature on small plates or as finger foods.

2 large red or yellow bell peppers, about 6 to 8 oz. each
1 tbs. full-flavored olive oil
¼ cup finely minced onion
2 cloves garlic, finely chopped
2 tbs. fresh fine breadcrumbs
1 tsp. paprika
½ tsp. dry mustard powder

½ tsp. dried marjoram
1 ½ tsp. sherry wine vinegar
salt and freshly ground pepper
½ cup finely chopped fresh parsley or cilantro
¼ cup grated manchego or Parmesan cheese, optional

Line a jelly-roll pan or cookie sheet with a piece of aluminum foil. Lightly oil foil. Divide peppers into sections by cutting along the natural depressions, usually 4 or 5 pieces. Remove ribs, seeds and curved ends to produce fairly flat strips. Gently flatten pepper strips with the palm of your hand. Place pepper strips skin-side down on a prepared pan. Preheat oven to 325°. Heat oil in a small skillet over medium heat. Add onion and cook for 5 minutes, or until soft. Add garlic and cook for another minute. Remove pan from heat and add breadcrumbs, paprika, mustard, marjoram, wine vinegar, salt, pepper and parsley. Mix well. Spoon a little of the onion mixture on each pepper strip. Bake peppers until very soft, about 35 to 40 minutes. Remove from oven and cut each strip into 2 or 3 pieces. Sprinkle with cheese if desired. Serve warm or at room temperature.

vegetables

TAPAS FANTÁSTICAS   **69**

Peppers with Tomato & Potato Stuffing

• MAKES 16 PIECES

Yellow and red bell peppers make a colorful platter. These can be made ahead of time and reheated just before serving. Serve warm or at room temperature on small plates.

4 small or 2 large red or yellow bell peppers, about 1 lb.
3 cups salted water for blanching
3 tbs. full-flavored olive oil
½ cup finely chopped onion
2 cloves garlic, minced
½ cup peeled, seeded, chopped tomatoes

1 cup diced cooked potatoes, in ¼-inch dice
1 tsp. dried marjoram
1 tbs. chopped fresh parsley
salt and freshly ground pepper
2 tbs. grated Parmesan cheese

❧ Cut small peppers in half lengthwise and then cut across each half. Remove stems, seeds and cores. Cut large peppers into quarters lengthwise along natural divisions, and cut each piece in half horizontally. Bring water to a boil in a medium saucepan. Blanch pepper pieces for 2 to 3 minutes to soften. Drain peppers and set aside.

❧ Preheat oven to 375°. Heat oil in a medium skillet over medium-high heat. Add onion and cook for 5 to 6 minutes, or until soft. Add garlic and tomatoes and cook 2 to 3 minutes. Remove from heat, and add potatoes, marjoram, parsley, salt and pepper. Mix well. Stuff each pepper piece with about 2 tablespoons of potato mixture and sprinkle with Parmesan cheese. Place peppers in one layer in an oiled shallow baking pan. Bake peppers until topping is lightly browned, about 20 to 25 minutes.

vegetables

70   TAPAS FANTÁSTICAS

Crisp Potato Slices

• Makes 4 to 6 servings

Simply baked potato slices are easy tapas. Use the thin slicing blade on the food processor to make thin, even slices. Arrange potatoes on cookie sheets ahead of time, and just pop them into the oven about 30 minutes before serving.

2 large baking potatoes
3 tbs. full-flavored olive oil

salt and freshly ground pepper

❧ Preheat oven to 350°. Line 2 large cookie sheets with aluminum foil and spray foil with nonstick cooking spray or oil lightly. Scrub potatoes. Cut off a thin slice from the end of each potato, and trim the sides if necessary to fit into a food processor tube. Slice into ⅛-inch slices. Pour olive oil, salt and pepper in a shallow pan or pie pan. Dip both sides of each slice in olive oil and place on prepared cookie sheets.

❧ Bake until slices are nicely browned and crisp, about 35 to 40 minutes. Remove slices as the edges start to turn dark brown. Serve hot or warm on a platter or in a paper-napkin-lined basket.

vegetables

Mini-Stuffed Potatoes

Small cooked red or Yukon gold potatoes are filled with a delectable onion and bacon stuffing. Cook potatoes and cool or refrigerate for easier handling. Stuff these ahead and bake just before serving.

1 lb. boiling potatoes, about 6
2 tbs. olive oil
⅓ cup finely chopped onion
1 tbs. sherry wine vinegar

2 tsp. Dijon mustard
salt and freshly ground pepper
3 slices cooked crisp bacon, crumbled
   into small pieces

❧ Scrub and cook unpeeled potatoes in boiling water until tender. Drain and cool. Cut potatoes in half. Using a small spoon or melon baller, scoop out potato centers, leaving a ¼-inch shell. Chop potato centers into pea-sized pieces and reserve.

❧ Preheat oven to 375°. Heat olive oil in a medium skillet over medium-low heat. Sauté onion for 5 to 6 minutes, or until very soft but not browned. Add vinegar, mustard and chopped potato centers to skillet, and season with salt and pepper. Cook for 2 to 3 minutes and stir until mixture is well combined. Remove from heat and stir in crumbled bacon. Divide stuffing among potato halves. Place in one layer on a cookie sheet or baking pan. Bake until filling is hot and shells are lightly browned and crisp, about 30 to 35 minutes.

vegetables

Oven-Roasted Baby Potatoes with Garlic

These very low-fat, vegetarian tapas can be served hot or warm. Have guests squeeze a roasted garlic clove onto their potatoes.

1 tbs. full-flavored olive oil
1 lb. small creamer potatoes, about
 1½-inch diameter
2 heads garlic, divided into cloves and
 unpeeled

1 tsp. coarse salt
freshly ground pepper

❧ Preheat oven to 400°. Line a shallow baking pan with foil and add olive oil. Wash and dry potatoes, and roll in olive oil to coat. Add garlic cloves and toss to coat with oil. Sprinkle potatoes and garlic with salt and pepper, rolling to coat all sides. Bake until potatoes are tender, about 35 to 40 minutes. Remove garlic cloves when brown and soft, about 20 to 25 minutes. Shake pan occasionally while roasting. Arrange on a serving plate with garlic cloves. Serve immediately.

vegetables

Spicy Baked Potato Wedges (Papas Bravas)

*This version of tapas is suggestive of French fries, but has less fat and more flavor. Dip the hot potato chunks in **Spicy Tomato Sauce**, page 147, or garlicky **Aïoli**, page 140, or as the Spaniards do, use a little of each.*

2 large baking potatoes, about 1½ lb., unpeeled
2 tbs. olive oil
2 tsp. mild chile powder, ground cumin or paprika

1 tsp. kosher or coarse sea salt
generous grinds black pepper

Preheat oven to 400°. Line a large cookie sheet with aluminum foil. Scrub potatoes and cut each in half horizontally. Place cut-side down on a cutting board and cut each half into 8 to 10 equal wedges and set aside. Combine oil, chile powder, salt and pepper. Add potatoes and toss to coat evenly with seasoned oil mixture. Place wedges skin-side down on a prepared baking sheet. Bake until potatoes are lightly browned, tender and lightly puffed, about 35 to 40 minutes. Serve on a heated platter with a bowl of sauce, or serve a few wedges on small plates with a spoonful of dipping sauce.

vegetables

Warm Potato and Leek Salad

Creamy, buttery Yukon gold potatoes are marvelous in this salad. Pour the dressing over warm potatoes for more flavor. Serve warm or at room temperature on small plates.

1 lb. small new potatoes, 1- to 1½-inch diameter
3 small leeks, or 1 large leek
¼ cup full-flavored olive oil, divided

2 tbs. sherry wine vinegar, divided
salt and freshly ground pepper
2 tbs. chopped parsley for garnish
paprika for garnish

❧ Scrub potatoes and place in a saucepan. Cover potatoes with water, bring to a boil and cook covered for 30 to 35 minutes, or until tender. When potatoes are tender, drain and place pot back over heat for another minute to dry out potatoes. As soon as potatoes are cool enough to handle, cut into quarters or slices and place in a serving bowl.

❧ While potatoes are cooking, cut leeks in half lengthwise and wash well to remove any sand. Remove 4 inches from the top of each leek and save for the stockpot or discard. Cut leek stalks into 1-inch pieces. Heat 1 tablespoon of the oil in a medium skillet over low heat. Add leeks and cook for 5 minutes. Add 1 tablespoon of the vinegar, salt and pepper. Cover and continue to cook for 5 to 10 minutes, or until tender. Remove from heat and place in a serving bowl.

❧ Whisk together remaining 3 tablespoons of oil, remaining 1 tablespoon of vinegar, salt and pepper, and pour over warm potatoes and leeks. Toss gently to keep potatoes in whole pieces. Sprinkle with parsley and a dust of paprika for garnish.

Variation: Add 2 or 3 strips of crisp bacon, crumbled.

vegetables

Russian-Style Vegetable Salad

Ensaladilla Rusa are flavorful tapas in Spain. These tapas probably arrived with the Frenchmen who came to Spain about the time of the Napoleonic wars. The basic salad always contains potatoes, carrots and peas. Beets, cauliflower and other cooked vegetables can also be added.

1 cup diced cooked potatoes, in ½-inch dice

1 cup diced cooked carrots, in ½-inch dice

1 cup frozen green peas, defrosted and cooked for 2 minutes

1 cup diced cooked turnip or celery root, in ½-inch dice

1 cup ½-inch pieces cooked green beans

5 to 6 green onions, white part only, finely chopped

salt and freshly ground pepper

¼ cup mayonnaise

2 tbs. sour cream

1 tbs. Dijon mustard

1 tbs. lemon juice

chopped fresh parsley

black olives or roasted red pepper strips for garnish

❧ Combine cooked vegetables with green onions. Season with salt and pepper. Combine mayonnaise, sour cream, mustard and lemon juice in a small bowl and mix well. Pour dressing over vegetables and toss until well coated. Cover and refrigerate until ready to serve. Spoon salad into a serving bowl or platter and sprinkle with parsley. Garnish with black olives or roasted red pepper strips.

vegetables

Mixed Grilled Vegetable Salad

Grilled vegetables or escalivada make appetizing tapas. Charcoal grilling gives eggplant and peppers a nice smoky flavor, but they can be cooked under the broiler as well. Serve on a platter, or layer a piece or two on a slice of toasted bread and top with a little bit of cheese.

3 red or yellow bell peppers
1 medium eggplant, or 4 to 5 Asian eggplants, about 1 lb., trimmed and cut into ¼-inch slices
1 to 2 portobello mushrooms, stem and gills removed
1 large red onion, cut into ½-inch slices
6 to 8 green onions, trimmed to include 3 to 4 inches of green top

3 to 4 zucchini or yellow squash, trimmed and cut into ¼-inch slices
¼ cup full-flavored olive oil, divided
salt and freshly ground black pepper
2 tsp. sherry wine vinegar
1 large ripe tomato, peeled, seeded and chopped

When ready to grill, place peppers over hottest area and char on all sides. Remove peppers and wrap in foil to steam for a few minutes before peeling. Brush eggplant, mushrooms, onions and squash slices generously with olive oil. Grill vegetables until nicely browned and tender over medium heat. Depending on heat source, eggplant slices will take about 10 to 12 minutes, onions 15 to 20 minutes, green onions and squash 8 to 10 minutes. Remove vegetables as they are cooked. Peel and seed peppers and cut into thin strips or 1-inch squares. Place in a serving bowl. Cut grilled vegetables into strips or squares and add peppers. Season with salt and pepper. Add remaining olive oil, vinegar and tomato pieces and toss to mix well. Serve warm or at room temperature.

Tip: If vegetables are browning too fast without becoming tender, remove from grill and microwave for 1 to 2 minutes to finish cooking.

vegetables

Spinach & Egg Empanadas

• MAKES FILLING FOR 16 (4½-INCH) OR
ABOUT 30 (2¾-INCH) EMPANADAS

Fill tender pastry rounds with this savory spinach mixture. Serve warm or at room temperature. These reheat well.

1 pkg. (10 oz.) frozen chopped spinach
2 tbs. butter
2 tbs. flour
½ cup milk
pinch nutmeg
1 tbs. Dijon mustard
salt and freshly ground pepper
pinch cayenne pepper
2 tsp. lemon juice

½ cup grated manchego or Gruyère cheese
2 hard-boiled eggs, peeled and chopped
5 to 6 green onions, white part only, thinly sliced
1 recipe *Easy Empanada Pastry*, page 150

❧Defrost spinach and drain well. Squeeze spinach with your hands to press out liquid, making spinach as dry as possible. Set aside in a bowl.

❧Heat butter in a medium saucepan over medium heat. When melted, add flour, stir to combine and cook for 1 minute. Add milk gradually and stir until sauce thickens. Add nutmeg and mustard, stirring to combine. Add well-drained spinach and cook for another 1 to 2 minutes. Season with salt, pepper and cayenne. Add lemon juice. Sauce will be quite thick. Remove from heat and stir in cheese, eggs and onions. Set aside to cool.

❧Assemble and bake empandas as instructed in the *Easy Empanada Pastry* recipe.

vegetables

Oven-Dried Tomatoes (Basic Recipe)

• Makes about ½ cup

*Oven-dried tomatoes become sweeter and their flavor intensifies when roasted in the oven. Use them in **Chicken, Artichoke & Oven-Dried Tomatoes**, page 110, **Pizzettes**, page 80, or **banderillas**, page 28.*

1 lb. plum tomatoes, about 4 or 5   salt and freshly ground pepper

Preheat oven to 250°. Line a shallow baking pan with aluminum foil. Remove core from tomatoes. Cut each in half, and then each half lengthwise into 3 or 4 pieces. Remove tomato seeds and any hard centers. Place tomatoes on a baking pan, skin-side down, and season with salt and pepper. Bake until tomatoes are dried but still pliable, about 2 hours. Remove from oven. When cool, store covered in the refrigerator for up to 4 or 5 days.

vegetables

Pizzettes with Vegetable Toppings

Pizza is more Italian than Spanish, but a thin, freshly baked bread crust provides the perfect foundation for many typical Spanish ingredients. The unbaked pizza crust in a tube from the supermarket refrigerator section makes a quick and easy base for a large variety of toppings. Prepare toppings while the crust pre-bakes, assemble and bake just before serving.

1 tube (10 oz.) unbaked pizza crust
Garlic Flavored Olive Oil, page 81

⅔ grated cheese, or **Toppings**, page 81

ᕦ Preheat oven to 375°. Remove dough from tube and carefully unroll. Place crust on the back of a lightly oiled cookie sheet or jelly-roll pan, and gently press the dough into a 10- by 15-inch rectangle. With a pizza wheel or sharp knife, cut dough into six 5-inch squares. Push in each edge of the pieces to form a slight ridge, forming 4-inch squares. Bake squares until crust is firm, but not browned, about 5 to 6 minutes. Top pizzettes with any of the toppings listed or create your own. Add a little olive oil and a thin layer of cheese. Several slices of the vegetables are also a perfect addition to the crisp thin crust. Do not overload.

ᕦ Final baking: Preheat oven to 425°. Bake until crust is brown around the edges and topping is bubbling, about 7 to 10 minutes. Cut each pizzette into 1-inch squares and serve immediately.

vegetables

Toppings

A thin layer of cheese provides flavor interest and helps to keep other ingredients from falling off.

Garlic-Flavored Oil

If desired, brush the prebaked crust with garlic-flavored oil before topping.

2 tbs. full-flavored olive oil

1 large clove garlic, minced

❧ Heat oil and garlic in a small skillet over medium-low heat. Cook for 1 to 2 minutes, or until garlic aroma is released. Do not allow garlic to brown. Or microwave oil and garlic in a small microwavable bowl on high for 30 seconds.

Other Toppings

Use any favorite cooked or grilled vegetables, including:

- Goat cheese, cream cheese, grated Monterey Jack, grated manchego or grated mozzarella
- *Sautéed Portabello Mushrooms*, page 65
- *Rainbow Peppers*, page 68
- Grilled eggplant

- *Wine & Garlic Chicken Nuggets*, page 114
- Thin slices cooked sausage
- Anchovies
- Baby clams and garlic
- *Spicy Tomato Sauce*, page 147, or *Romesco Sauce*, page 144

Pizzettes with Vegetable Toppings

seafood
tapas

Steamed Mussels with Parsley Sauce, page 95

82   TAPAS FANTÁSTICAS

Seafood ranks high on the list of favorite Spanish tapas and there are innumerable ways to prepare shrimp, calamari, clams, shellfish and fish. In addition to its wide availability and popularity, seafood cooks quickly. It is important to always buy the freshest and highest quality available and to not overcook seafood. Some of our favorite tapas include *Stuffed Clams with Spinach*, *Steamed Mussels with Parsley Sauce*, *Scallops with Oranges & Black Olives* and *Hot Garlic Shrimp*.

Salt cod is a typical Spanish ingredient and must be soaked at least 24 hours to remove excess salt and soften. Try the *Salt Cod & Potato Cakes* and the *Garlicky Salt Cod-Topped Potato Slices* when the cod has been prepared for cooking. There are several flavorful sauces in the *Basic Sauces & Pastry* chapter to complement cooked shellfish and fish, so make some delicious seafood tapas for your next party.

Fried Calamari

*Crisp, hot fried calamari is delicious Serve with **Aïoli**, page 140, **Seafood Cocktail Sauce**, page 145, or **Romesco Sauce**, page 144. The calamari can be cleaned and prepared ahead of time, but should be floured and fried at the last minute and served immediately.*

1 lb. calamari or squid, cleaned
½ cup cake flour
1 tsp. paprika

½ tsp. dry mustard powder
salt and freshly ground pepper
3 cups canola oil

❧ Cut calamari into ½-inch rings. If using tentacles, remove and discard any hard pieces in the middle. Combine flour, paprika, mustard, salt and pepper on a large shallow plate. Preheat oven to 275°. Heat oil in a heavy pan until oil reaches 375° on a thermometer. Dredge calamari lightly in the flour mixture and shake off excess flour. Add about ¼ of the calamari to the hot oil and fry until a light golden brown, about 1 to 2 minutes. Remove to a paper towel-lined platter and place in the oven until the next batch is fried. Allow oil temperature to return to 375° and continue to fry remaining calamari. Serve hot.

seafood

Calamari Cocktail

It only takes a couple of minutes to cook calamari and it tends to toughen when overcooked. Cooked calamari can be moistened with our zippy **Seafood Cocktail Sauce**, *page 45, and served in small lettuce cups or on small plates with crackers.*

2 to 3 quarts water
1 tsp. salt
1 lb. calamari, cleaned, cut into thin
    rings and dried between paper towels
½ to ¼ cup *Seafood Cocktail Sauce*

chopped fresh cilantro or parsley for
    garnish
8 to 10 small black olives for garnish
small lettuce leaves

Bring 2 to 3 quarts water to a boil in a large saucepan. Add salt and calamari and blanch for 2 to 3 minutes. The calamari is cooked properly when it turns white and loses its translucency. Immediately drain and pat dry with paper towels. Place calamari in a serving bowl, pour cocktail sauce over and mix well. If not serving calamari immediately, cover and refrigerate. Remove from refrigerator about 30 minutes before serving. Garnish with cilantro or parsley and black olives. Serve at room temperature in a seafood cocktail glass; or let your guests fill a lettuce cup, roll it up and eat.

seafood

Stuffed Clams with Spinach

Cooked clams are combined with a savory spinach filling and served hot in their shells. A good way to keep clams upright during baking is to place a layer of rock salt in a baking pan.

1 recipe *Steamed Clams*, page 87, about 20 with strained juice
¼ cup butter, divided
3 green onions, white part only, finely chopped
1 tbs. flour
¼ cup milk

1 pkg. (10 oz.) spinach, defrosted, squeezed very dry and finely chopped
salt and freshly ground pepper
pinch nutmeg
1 cup fresh breadcrumbs
2 cloves garlic, finely chopped

❧ Remove clams from their shells, coarsely chop and set aside. Strain the liquid from the bottom of the pan through a coffee filter to remove any sand and garlic pieces, and reserve ¼ cup liquid. Melt 2 tablespoons of butter in a small saucepan over medium-high heat. Add onions and sauté for 2 to 3 minutes, or until soft. Stir in flour and cook for 1 minute. Add ¼ cup of reserved clam juice and milk and bring to a boil. Lower heat and cook for 2 to 3 minutes. Stir in spinach, chopped clams, salt, pepper and nutmeg. Mix well. Fill each clamshell halfway with spinach filling and place on a baking pan.

❧ Preheat oven to 400°. Melt remaining 2 tablespoons of butter in a small skillet. When foamy, add fresh breadcrumbs. Cook over medium heat until breadcrumbs are lightly browned. Add garlic and cook for another minute. Sprinkle a few toasted crumbs over each stuffed clam. Bake until hot, about 15 minutes. Serve immediately or place on a warming tray.

seafood

Steamed Clams

MAKES 20 PIECES

*Serve these clams warm or at room temperature with **Red Pepper Mayonnaise**, page 143, **Sherry Vinegar and Shallot Sauce**, page 146, or **Parsley Sauce**, page 142, or use them for **Stuffed Clams with Spinach**, page 86. Double this recipe if you are serving a large group.*

2 lbs. cherrystone or Manilla clams, about 20
½ cup water
½ cup dry white wine
3 cloves garlic, coarsely chopped

❧ Rinse clams in a bowl of cold water. Fill a bowl with cold water, add 1 tablespoon of kosher or sea salt, and allow clams to stand for 1 hour to release any sand. Lift clams from water and discard any clams that are not tightly closed.

❧ To steam clams, add water, wine and garlic to a deep saucepan with a tight-fitting lid. Bring water to a boil and add clams. Cover tightly and steam over high heat. After 3 to 4 minutes, remove the clams that have opened and place on a plate or bowl. Continue to steam unopened clams. Check again in 2 to 3 minutes, removing opened clams. Re-cover pan and turn off heat. After 5 minutes, discard any unopened clams and save cooking liquid. When clams are cool enough to handle, discard top shell. Serve clams in a small bowl with sauce on the side; or take a small knife and loosen the clam from its bottom shell and spoon a dollop of sauce on each clam. Strain clam liquid by pouring though a coffee filter or cheesecloth to catch any sand. Use liquid as directed in recipe.

seafood

Basic salt cod preparation

One pound dried salt cod makes approximately 2 cups cooked, flaked fish.

❧ Start soaking the dried salt cod a day before you want to cook it. After soaking, cod will keep in the refrigerator for 3 or 4 days. Rinse fish pieces under cold running water for a few minutes to wash off as much salt as possible.

❧ Place cod pieces in a large bowl, cover with cold water and soak for 10 minutes. Drain, cover with cold water and soak again for 10 minutes. Repeat this process 4 or 5 times. Cover cod with fresh cold water, cover bowl and refrigerate for 24 hours. Change water 1 to 2 times during this soaking period. Water should only taste slightly salty after this soaking.

❧ Drain cod, place in a large saucepan, cover with cold water and bring to a boil. Reduce heat, cover and simmer for 20 to 25 minutes, or until fish flakes easily. Drain. When cool enough to handle, flake or chop fish as directed in recipe.

seafood

Salt Cod & Potato Cakes

*Serve these small hot crispy cakes with a dollop of **Aïoli**, page 140, or **Parsley Sauce**, page 142. Leftover mashed potatoes or instant mashed potatoes work well in this dish. The cakes can be made ahead of time and kept warm in the oven or reheated for a few seconds in the microwave.*

2 tbs. olive oil plus more for frying
¼ cup finely chopped green onions, white part only
1 cup finely chopped prepared cooked salt cod, about ½-inch pieces

¾ cup prepared mashed potatoes
white pepper and salt
1 egg yolk
fine dry breadcrumbs

Heat oil in a medium skillet over medium heat. Sauté onion for 3 to 4 minute, or until soft but do not brown. Remove from heat and reserve. Combine cod and potatoes in a bowl. Taste for seasoning, add white pepper and salt if needed. Stir in egg yolk, onions and oil from skillet. Mix well. Form into small patties, about 1½-inch diameter and ½-inch thick. Lightly coat each cake with breadcrumbs.

Add enough olive oil to cover bottom of skillet, about ¼-inch deep. Heat oil over medium-high heat. When hot, fry cakes until lightly brown and heated through. Drain on paper towels. Serve immediately.

seafood

Garlicky Salt Cod-Topped Potato Slices

This goes together quickly when you have cooked potatoes and some soaked, cooked salt cod in the refrigerator. It is easier to slice potatoes after they have cooled and refrigerated.

4 to 5 small boiling potatoes, red,
   Finnish or Yukon gold, about
   1½- to 2-inches diameter
salt to taste
1 cup flaked, cooked salt cod,
   page 88, about 5 oz.

¼ cup *Aïoli*, page 140
finely chopped parsley or cilantro to
   taste for garnish
roasted red pepper or pimiento strips
   for garnish

❧Scrub potatoes, but do not peel. Boil in salted water until tender, but not mushy. Drain potatoes and cool. Slice cooked potatoes into rounds about ⅜-inches thick. Combine flaked cod with aioli and parsley in a small bowl. Top each potato slice with a generous tablespoon of salt cod mixture and garnish with a thin strip of roasted red pepper. These can be assembled 1 to 2 hours ahead. Remove from the refrigerator about 30 minutes before serving.

Variation: Cut 2 hard-boiled eggs into thin slices. To assemble, place an egg slice on top of each potato slice, lightly season with salt and pepper and top with salt cod mixture.

seafood

Monkfish in Tomato Almond Sauce

• Makes 4 to 6 servings

Monkfish is a flavorful, dense-textured fish that some find to be similar to lobster. Halibut, swordfish or cod make good substitutes. Prepare the tomato sauce first and bake the fish for a few minutes. Serve hot on small plates or spear chunks with a toothpick.

2 tbs. full-flavored olive oil
1 slice bread, about ¾-inch thick, crust removed
10 blanched almonds
1 clove garlic, chopped
2 large ripe tomatoes, peeled, seeded and chopped, about 1 cup

pinch saffron threads or powder
2 tbs. lemon juice
⅓ cup water
salt and white pepper
1 lb. monkfish or other firm-fleshed fish, cut into 1-inch cubes
chopped fresh parsley for garnish

Preheat oven to 375°. Heat oil in a medium, ovenproof skillet over medium heat. Tear bread into several pieces and add to skillet. Add almonds and sauté, stirring, until bread and almonds are lightly browned. Add garlic and cook for another minute, but do not allow to brown. Add tomato, saffron and lemon juice, reduce heat and simmer for a few minutes. Pour into a food processor or blender bowl with water, and process until fairly smooth. Add salt and pepper to taste.

Pour sauce back into the skillet. Sauce will be thick, but monkfish liquid will be released as it cooks. Bring to a boil and remove from heat. Salt and pepper monkfish, and add monkfish chunks to skillet. Toss to coat fish with sauce. Place skillet in the oven and bake for 15 minutes, turning fish over about halfway through cooking time. Sprinkle with parsley for garnish and serve hot.

seafood

Escabèche

This piquant seafood dish can be prepared a day or two ahead of time. Firm-fleshed fish such as halibut, orange roughy or sea bass can be substituted. Serve on small plates with forks or cut fish into bite-sized pieces. Serve with toothpicks.

1 lb. red snapper fillets
flour for dusting fish
3 tbs. olive oil, divided
1 medium onion, thinly sliced
1 small carrot, peeled and thinly sliced
3 cloves garlic, peeled and thinly sliced
⅛ tsp. dried red pepper flakes
½ cup cider vinegar
¼ cup water

1 tsp. brown sugar
1 tbs. lemon juice
2 sprigs fresh thyme, or ½ tsp. dried thyme
salt and pepper to taste
2 tbs. white raisins
1 tbs. capers, drained and rinsed
black olives for garnish

Cut each fish fillet into 2 to 3 medium pieces. Season pieces generously with salt and pepper and dust lightly with flour. Heat a large skillet over medium heat and add 2 tablespoons of the olive oil. Quickly sauté fish for 3 to 4 minutes on each side, or until lightly browned and cooked through. Remove fish and place one layer in a deep-sided glass or nonreactive pan. Discard hot oil, wipe out skillet, add remaining 1 tablespoon of olive oil to skillet and heat over medium heat. Add onion, carrots, garlic and red pepper flakes. Cook for 2 to 3 minutes, or until onion and carrot soften. Add vinegar, water, brown sugar, lemon juice, thyme, raisins, salt and pepper to skillet. Bring to a boil and cook for 2 to 3 minutes. Pour over fish. Sprinkle with capers, cool to room temperature, cover and refrigerate for a few hours or overnight. Before serving, bring to room temperature and garnish with black olives.

seafood

Seafood Salad

This simply cooked and lightly dressed dish is totally dependent on the quality of the seafood and tomatoes. Serve on small plates at cool room temperature.

3 tbs. olive oil
1 tbs. sherry wine vinegar
1 tbs. lemon juice
salt and white pepper to taste
1 tbs. capers, drained and finely chopped
1 tbs. kosher salt
¼ lb. small white shrimp, peeled and deveined

¼ lb. small bay scallops
¼ lb. calamari, cleaned and cut into ¼-inch rings
¼ lb. firm-fleshed halibut, flounder or sole, cut into ½-inch cubes
1 tbs. chopped fresh parsley
1 hard-boiled egg, finely chopped
½ cup peeled, seeded, chopped ripe tomato

❧ Prepare dressing in a serving bowl by whisking together olive oil, wine vinegar, lemon juice, salt and pepper. Add capers. Bring at least 2 quarts of water to boil in a large pot. Add kosher salt. On a tray or cookie sheet, place 2 or 3 layers of paper towels. Place shrimp in a basket or strainer with a handle, and hold in the boiling water for 1 to 2 minutes, or until shrimp turn opaque. Shake and drain shrimp and pour onto paper towels. Drain on paper towels for a minute and place in a serving bowl with the dressing. Toss to combine. Repeat cooking with scallops, calamari and white fish. Drain before placing in a serving bowl. Just before serving, add parsley, egg and tomato and taste. Add salt and pepper if necessary and toss to combine.

seafood

Basic Steamed Mussels

Blacked-shelled mussels make attractive as well as delicious tapas. Steamed mussels can be served in small bowls with a little of their strained cooking broth, or loosen them from their shells.

1 lb. mussels
1 lemon, thinly sliced
1 large shallot, finely chopped
1 bay leaf
dried red pepper flakes

2 to 3 fresh parsley sprigs
1 fresh thyme sprig
⅓ cup dry white wine or vermouth
1 ½ cups water

To prepare live mussels, place them in a bowl of cold water and soak them for 10 to 15 minutes. Wash shells under cold running water and scrub mussels with a small brush. Pull off beards, which are small strings protruding from the shells. Squeeze the shell of any open mussel and if it does not close tightly, discard it. If a mussel seems particularly heavy for its size, it may be full of sand, so discard it as well. In a tall pot, combine lemon slices, shallots, bay leaf, red pepper flakes, parsley, thyme, wine and water. Bring to a boil, cover and simmer for 3 to 4 minutes. Add cleaned mussels, cover and steam over high heat for 3 to 5 minutes, or until most of the mussels have opened. The pot has a tendency to boil over, so watch carefully and lift the lid for a few seconds once or twice during cooking. Remove mussels from the pot and discard any mussels that do not open. Place in individual bowls or one large bowl and strain broth over mussels. Serve hot.

Variation: Top with a little *Sherry Vinegar & Shallot Sauce*, page 146, *Parsley Sauce*, page 142, pesto or your favorite salsa.

seafood

Steamed Mussels with Parsley Sauce

Steamed mussels are topped with a tangy green sauce and served warm or at room temperature. The precooked, frozen New Zealand green-lipped mussels can be substituted in this recipe. Defrost and heat them according to package directions and top with sauce.

seafood

1 lb. *Basic Steamed Mussels*, page 94

½ cup *Parsley Sauce*, page 142

∾ Remove steamed mussels from pot. Discard top shell and loosen mussels from the bottom shell with a small knife. Top with a teaspoon of *Parsley Sauce* and arrange on a serving platter. Serve warm or at room temperature.

Mussels Stuffed with Garlic & Breadcrumbs

Make a savory topping of garlic and breadcrumbs, and broil the mussels for a few minutes before serving. Serve on small plates with forks. Be sure to loosen the mussels from their shells for easier eating.

1 lb. *Basic Steamed Mussels*, page 94
1 tbs. olive oil
1 clove garlic, finely chopped
⅛ tsp. dried red pepper flakes
½ tsp. dried marjoram or thyme

1 cup fresh breadcrumbs
grated zest from 1 lemon
1 tablespoon chopped fresh parsley
salt and freshly ground pepper
¼ cup dry white wine

❧Preheat broiler. Discard top shell, and with a small knife loosen each mussel from the bottom shell. Place on a baking sheet. Heat oil in a medium skillet over medium heat. Sauté garlic and red pepper flakes over low heat for 2 to 3 minutes, or until garlic softens. Add marjoram, breadcrumbs, lemon zest and parsley. Season with salt and pepper and mix well. Firmly press about 2 teaspoons of breadcrumb mixture onto each mussel. Sprinkle each mussel with about ½ teaspoon of white wine. Position broiler rack about 6 inches from heat source. Broil mussels for 3 to 5 minutes, or until topping has lightly browned. Serve warm or at room temperature.

seafood

Bacon & Green Onion-Stuffed Mussels

❧ Omit olive oil and garlic in *Mussels Stuffed with Garlic & Breadcrumbs*. Substitute 1 slice of bacon cut into ¼-inch pieces. Sauté in a skillet until crisp. Remove bacon and add 2 finely chopped green onions, cooking until soft. Continue as in *Mussels Stuffed with Garlic & Breadcrumbs,* page 96.

Pesto-Topped Mussels

❧ Mix 2 tablespoons of prepared pesto with 1 cup of fresh breadcrumbs. Press mixture over mussels, sprinkle each with a little white wine and broil.

Smoked Salmon & Cucumber Tartlets

• MAKES ABOUT 12 TARTLETS

Spread this appetizing filling on crackers if you don't have time to make tart shells. Filling can be made 1 to 2 hours ahead. Remove from the refrigerator at least 30 minutes before filling the shells.

½ cup diced peeled, seeded cucumber, in ¼-inch dice
4 oz. smoked salmon, cut into ¼-inch dice
3 tbs. whipped cream cheese
1 tsp. lemon juice

½ tsp. dried tarragon
1 tbs. finely chopped fresh mint leaves
pinch of white pepper
12 tartlets from *Basic Tartlet Pastry*, page 152, baked and cooled

Drain diced cucumber on paper towels for 20 minutes to absorb any liquid. Combine cucumber, smoked salmon, cream cheese, lemon juice, tarragon, mint and white pepper. Stir until well combined. Spoon mixture into baked tart shells and serve immediately.

seafood

Sardine & Egg Empanadas

Serve this full-flavored sardine and egg filled empanada slightly warm or at room temperature. A copita of dry sherry or a glass of white wine is a perfect accompaniment.

1 can (5 oz.) sardines, oil-packed, drained and flaked
2 hard-boiled eggs, peeled and chopped
1 tbs. capers, rinsed, drained, dried and coarsely chopped

4 tsp. Dijon mustard
generous grinds black pepper
1 recipe *Easy Empanada Pastry*, page 150, or *Basic Empanada Pastry*, page 148

❧ Combine sardines, eggs, capers and mustard; stir well. Season with pepper. Fill and bake empanadas as directed in the pastry recipe.

Baked empanadas can be frozen. Preheat oven to 350°. Place frozen empanadas on a cookie sheet and bake until hot, about 15 to 20 minutes. If empanadas have been refrigerated, reheat until warm to the touch, about 7 to 10 minutes.

seafood

Lemon Scallops

Use medium-sized sea scallops and serve hot on small plates with forks or toothpicks. The lemon and capers add some punch to this popular shellfish.

1 lb. sea scallops
salt and freshly ground pepper
2 tbs. olive oil
½ cup minced shallots
zest and juice of 1 lemon

3 tbs. dry white wine
1 tbs. capers, rinsed, drained and
    coarsely chopped
¼ cup chopped fresh Italian parsley

❧ Remove and discard tough muscle from the sides of the scallops. Wash and pat dry and season with salt and pepper. Preheat a large nonstick skillet over medium heat. Add olive oil. Place scallops in a skillet, sauté for 2 minutes and turn over. Add shallots to a pan and cook for another 2 minutes. Remove scallops to a plate; set aside. Add lemon juice and zest, white wine and capers. Increase heat to high and reduce liquid to a thin sauce for 2 minutes. Return scallops to the pan and toss with the sauce. Sprinkle with parsley and serve in a heated bowl.

seafood

Scallops with Oranges and Black Olives

• MAKES 6 SERVINGS

Orange segments and red onion slices accent these shellfish tapas. If made ahead of time, remove from the refrigerator about 30 minutes before serving. Serve on small plates with forks.

2 navel oranges
1 lb. large sea scallops, about 10 to 12
salt and freshly ground black pepper
1 tsp. olive oil
2 tsp. white wine vinegar or lemon juice

2 tbs. frozen orange juice concentrate, undiluted
1 small red onion, thinly sliced into rings
½ cup imported black olives for garnish

❧ Using a citrus zester, cut long strips of zest from 1 orange, or use a potato peeler to remove strips. Cut the strips into long matchsticks with a sharp knife. Set aside. Cut a thin slice from the top and bottom of each orange. With a sharp, thin-bladed knife, cutting from top to bottom, remove the peel and membrane under it to expose the fruit. Cut down on each side of the membranes to release the segments. Set segments aside. Squeeze any juice remaining in the membranes into a small bowl and add zest, vinegar and juice concentrate.

❧ Remove small tough muscle from sides of scallops and discard. Wash and dry scallops and generously season with salt and pepper. Heat a nonstick skillet over high heat. Add oil and scallops, and sear for 1 to 2 minutes on each side, or until lightly browned. Remove scallops and place on a plate. Add orange juice mixture and onion rings to pan and stir for a minute. Add orange segments and combine. Return scallops to the pan and cook for 1 to 2 minutes. Pour into a serving dish. Taste for seasoning and garnish with black olives. Serve warm or at room temperature.

seafood

Shrimp A La Plancha

After marinating for a few minutes, these shrimp are sautéed in a hot skillet. Shrimp served in their shells are more difficult to eat, but are very flavorful and moist. Serve warm.

1 lb. large shrimp, about 30 to 35,
   peeled and deveined
2 tbs. olive oil

3 tbs. lemon juice, divided
2 cloves garlic, finely minced
salt and freshly ground pepper

❧ Dry and skewer shrimp pinwheel-style, (see photo opposite page). With a cocktail pick or a short 3-inch skewer, pierce the tail of one shrimp, go through the thick end of the second shrimp, then through the thick end of the first shrimp and then the tail of the second. You should have a circular form that has almost uniform thickness. Mix together oil, 2 tablespoons lemon juice, garlic, salt and pepper on a large plate. Dip shrimp in this marinade, coating both sides, and marinate on plate for about 15 minutes. Preheat a large cast iron or heavy skillet over high heat. When skillet is very hot, a drop of water will evaporate immediately. Lift shrimp skewers from the marinade and place in a skillet. Press shrimp down firmly with a spatula and cook for 2 minutes on each side, or until just barely cooked through. Sprinkle with the remaining lemon juice and serve immediately.

Variation: To serve shrimp in their shells, cut down the back of each shrimp with a sharp knife and fish out the dark vein. Skewer and marinate, making sure some of the marinade gets under the shells. Sauté as directed above.

seafood

Shrimp A La Plancha, page 102

Hot Garlic Shrimp

Make these tapas with the highest quality shrimp you can find. This recipe works well with any size shrimp, just cook larger shrimp a minute or two longer. Serve warm or at room temperature in a small, shallow bowl with toothpicks.

3 tbs. lemon juice
¼ tsp. green or red Tabasco Sauce
2 tsp. sugar
salt to taste
3 tbs. full-flavored olive oil

1 lb. medium white shrimp, peeled and deveined
3 cloves garlic, finely chopped
1 tbs. fresh chopped parsley or cilantro for garnish

❧ Combine lemon juice, Tabasco, sugar and salt. Set aside. Heat oil in a nonstick skillet over medium heat. Add shrimp and garlic. Stir-fry for 1 to 2 minutes. When shrimp start to turn opaque, add lemon juice mixture. Continue to cook and stir until shrimp are barely cooked through. Remove shrimp with a slotted spoon and place on a serving dish. Reduce pan juices over high heat until thick and syrupy. Pour over shrimp and sprinkle with parsley or cilantro. Place in a serving dish and serve immediately.

seafood

Broiled Shrimp with Bacon

Here is another party favorite. The shrimp can be assembled ahead of time, and broiled just before serving. Use very thinly sliced bacon to wrap the shrimp, and secure with toothpicks, if bacon does not stay in place. Serve hot or warm with toothpicks.

1 lb. large shrimp, about 25 to 30, peeled and deveined
¼ cup Dijon mustard

freshly ground pepper
8 strips bacon, thinly sliced

❧ Preheat broiler. Dry shrimp. Spread a little mustard on each side of the shrimp and season with ground pepper. Cut each bacon slice in half crosswise, and half again lengthwise to make 4 thin strips. Wind a bacon piece around each shrimp and place on the broiler rack. Position shrimp about 6 inches from the heat source. Broil for 3 minutes, turn shrimp over and cook 2 to 3 minutes, or until bacon is crisp and shrimp just barely cooked through. Do not overcook.

Smoked Trout in Endive Leaves

Endive leaves filled with a horseradish-flavored cream and topped with pieces of smoked trout make elegant, light tapas. If they are available, use both red and white endive. Smoked salmon can be substituted for the trout.

½ cup sour cream or crème fraiche
1 tsp. prepared horseradish
salt and a generous grind white pepper
5 oz. smoked trout

20 to 24 red or white Belgian endive leaves, about 2 heads
1 tbs. chopped fresh parsley or small watercress leaves for garnish

❧ Combine sour cream, horseradish, salt and pepper. Remove any skin and bones from the trout, and cut or break into 1-inch-long x ½-inch-wide pieces to fit into the endive leaves. Cut off bottom end of endive head and separate the leaves. Spoon a little horseradish cream into the larger end of the endive, top with a piece of trout and put a little more cream on top of the trout. Repeat with remaining endive leaves. Garnish with parsley or watercress. These can be done 1 hour ahead and refrigerated until ready to serve.

seafood

Tuna & Egg Tartlets

Bake tartlet shells a day or two ahead, and keep them in an airtight container. The filling can also be made ahead and refrigerated. Anchovy paste is available in tubes at most supermarkets.

1 can (6 ½ oz.) oil-packed tuna, drained
1 hard-boiled egg, chopped
3 tbs. capers, rinsed, drained and
   chopped
2 tsp. Dijon mustard
2 tsp. mayonnaise

1 tsp. anchovy paste
freshly ground pepper
2 tbs. chopped fresh parsley
½ recipe baked *Basic Tartlet Pastry*,
   page 152

❧ Combine tuna, egg, capers, mustard, mayonnaise and anchovy paste. Mix well, season with pepper and stir in parsley. If filling has been refrigerated, remove it from the refrigerator about 30 minutes before assembling tarts. Just before serving, fill each tartlet shell with about 1 tablespoon of filling. Serve at room temperature.

seafood

tapas poultry

A variety of delicious chicken dishes can be found on the tapas table. Many of your favorite recipes can be served as tapas if the meat is cut into smaller pieces and served with toothpicks, forks or as finger foods. Chicken salads, grilled chicken legs or wings, and chunks of chicken cooked in a savory orange, tomato or barbecue sauces are all candidates for the tapas table. We include recipes for an appetizing *Chicken, Artichoke & Oven-Dried Tomatoes* dish that can be prepared just before your guests arrive. The *Goat Cheese, Eggplant & Tomato-Stuffed Chicken Breasts* are braised and cut into slices to show off their colorful filling. Fast and easy *Wine & Garlic Chicken Nuggets* are made with chicken thighs and always a crowd-pleaser. *Lentil & Duck Salad* gets a quick start by using a duck from your favorite Chinese deli or take-out. Whether you start from scratch or buy already prepared ingredients, you'll want to include at least one poultry dish on your tapas table.

Goat Cheese, Eggplant & Tomato-Stuffed Chicken Breasts, page 113

Chicken, Artichoke &
Oven-Dried Tomatoes

*This tapas dish
is both colorful
and flavorful.
Serve warm or
at room tem-
perature on
small plates
with forks. The
chicken is easily
sliced if placed
in the freezer
for 30 minutes.*

2 to 3 boneless, skinless, chicken
    breast halves, about 1 lb.
2 tbs. full-flavored olive oil
2 tbs. lemon juice
½ tsp. dried marjoram

1 pkg. (8 oz.) frozen artichoke hearts
½ cup *Oven-Dried Tomatoes*, page 79,
    cut into ½-inch pieces
3 green onions, white part only, minced
salt and freshly ground pepper

❧ Wash and dry chicken breasts. With a sharp knife, slice chicken diagonally across the grain to yield ¼-inch thick medallions, about 1½-inch square. Mix together oil, lemon juice and marjoram. Add chicken pieces and marinate for 15 minutes. Cook artichoke hearts according to package directions, drain and set aside.

❧ Preheat a large nonstick skillet over medium-high heat. Add chicken marinade, salt and pepper to pan. Stir-fry for 3 minutes until chicken is cooked through but not brown. Add artichokes, tomato pieces and green onions and toss to combine. Arrange on a serving platter. Adjust seasoning and add more lemon juice or olive oil if desired. Serve warm or at cool room temperature.

poultry

Velvet Chicken Breast Chunks

*Everyone loves these succulent morsels and they only take a few minutes to prepare. Sauce the chunks with **Almond Sauce**, page 141, **Romesco Sauce**, page 144, or **Parsley Sauce**, page 142.*

2 to 3 boneless, skinless, chicken breast
   halves, about 1 lb.
½ cup flour
1 tbs. paprika
½ tsp. salt
⅛ tsp. white pepper
1 tbs. olive oil
½-¾ cup *Almond Sauce* or *Romesco Sauce*
parsley for garnish

❧ Preheat oven to 375°. Cut chicken into 20 to 24 equal chunks. Pat dry with paper towels. Combine flour, paprika, salt and pepper in a paper bag. Add chicken and shake to coat pieces evenly. Preheat a large nonstick skillet over medium heat and add olive oil. Shake excess flour from chicken pieces and place in skillet. Lightly brown on one side, turn, and brown other side. Place skillet in oven until chicken is barely cooked through, about 7 to 8 minutes.

❧ While chicken is in oven, add *Almond* or *Romesco Sauce* to a medium saucepan and gently heat. The sauce should have a pourable consistency, so thin with a little stock or water if necessary. Lift chicken pieces from skillet and place in sauce. Stir gently to combine and simmer for 1 to 2 minutes. Turn into a preheated serving dish and garnish with parsley. Serve hot or warm on small plates with forks or on toothpicks.

poultry

Chicken & Carrots with Orange Sherry Sauce

• MAKES 4 TO 6 SERVINGS

It takes just a few minutes to stir-fry the chicken breasts and finish in a delicious orange sherry sauce. Serve on small plates with forks or toothpicks.

½ lb. baby carrots or 3 medium carrots
1 tsp. salt for cooking water
2-3 boneless, skinless, chicken breast
   halves, about 1 lb.
1 tbs. olive oil
salt and freshly ground pepper

¼ cup minced shallots
zest from 1 orange
¼ cup orange juice
1 tsp. sherry wine vinegar
¼ cup medium dry sherry
¼ tsp. dry mustard powder

❧ Peel, trim tops and tail, and cut baby carrots into 1-inch lengths, or cut whole carrots into diagonal slices about ½-inch thick. Bring water to a boil in a small saucepan, add salt and blanch carrots until crisp-tender, about 2 to 3 minutes. Drain carrots and reserve.

❧ Trim any remaining fat from chicken breasts and cut into 20 to 24 equal pieces. Pat dry with a paper towel. Heat oil in a large nonstick skillet over medium-high heat. Add chicken, season with salt and pepper, and sauté for 2 to 3 minutes, or until chicken pieces turn opaque. Add shallots and cook for another minute. Add orange zest, orange juice, vinegar, sherry, mustard and carrots. Reduce heat, cover and cook for 6 to 8 minutes more, or until chicken is cooked through and sauce has reduced. Pour into a serving bowl. Serve hot or warm.

poultry

Goat Cheese, Eggplant & Tomato-Stuffed Chicken Breasts

Chicken breasts are pounded flat and stuffed with a colorful, zesty filling. Cooked carrots or potatoes can be substituted for the eggplant. These can be done ahead of time and refrigerated before serving. Serve on small plates with forks.

3 small boneless, skinless, chicken
   breast halves, about 1 lb.
¼ cup creamy goat cheese
¼ cup coarsely chopped cooked eggplant
3 to 4 green onions, white part only,
   minced

3 tbs. chopped *Oven-Dried Tomatoes*,
   page 79, or sun-dried tomatoes,
   oil-packed
salt and freshly ground pepper
1 tsp. full-flavored olive oil
¼ cup medium sherry

∾ Trim any remaining fat from chicken breasts. If still attached, remove the tenderloin and save for another purpose. Place each breast half between two sheets of plastic wrap, and flatten with a meat mallet until it is a uniform ¼-inch thickness, about 4- by 8-inches in size.

∾ Combine goat cheese, eggplant, onions and tomatoes. Season mixture and chicken breasts with salt and pepper. Spread each flattened breast with ⅓ of the filling, bringing it within 1 inch of the straightest long edge. Roll up the long side like a jelly roll. After the first turn, fold in the two ends and continue rolling tightly. Pin with toothpicks at each end to hold roll together.

∾ Heat olive oil in a medium skillet over medium-high heat. Place chicken rolls seam-side down in skillet. Turn to brown on all sides, about 5 minutes total. Add sherry to skillet, cover tightly, reduce heat and braise for 10 minutes. Remove to a plate and cool for 15 minutes. Slice into ¾-inch slices. Serve cool at room temperature.

poultry

Wine & Garlic Chicken Nuggets

Chunks of chicken thighs are stir-fried with lots of garlic to make this appetizing, quick tapa.

2 lb. chicken thighs, about 6
1 tbs. full-flavored olive oil
6 cloves garlic, thinly sliced, about 3 tbs.
½ cup full-bodied red wine
¼ tsp. Tabasco Sauce

salt to taste
1 tbs. lemon juice
¼ cup chopped fresh cilantro or parsley
  for garnish

❧ Remove bone, skin and excess fat from chicken thighs and save to make chicken stock. Cut each thigh into 6 to 8 equal pieces. Heat oil in a medium skillet over medium heat. Add garlic slices and soften in oil for 2 to 3 minutes, but do not brown. Add chicken pieces and increase heat to high. Stir-fry chicken until it firms and changes color. Add wine, Tabasco and salt. Cover, reduce heat to medium and simmer for 2 to 3 minutes. Remove lid, increase heat to high and reduce sauce to a thick glaze. Add lemon juice and cilantro or parsley. Serve warm on small plates or in a shallow bowl with toothpicks.

poultry

Rice- & Chicken-Stuffed Tomatoes

If you have cooked chicken and rice in the refrigerator, this savory dish goes together quickly. Serve warm on small plates with forks.

4 medium tomatoes, about 2½- to 3-inch diameter
1 tbs. olive oil
⅓ cup finely chopped onion
pinch saffron or turmeric
1 clove garlic , finely chopped

½ tsp. dried marjoram
¾ cup cooked rice
¾ cup diced cooked chicken
salt and freshly ground pepper
2 tbs. chopped parsley

❧ Cut tomatoes in half through stem. Carefully trim stem end. Scoop out centers and seeds of each tomato half. Discard seeds and chop removed tomato pulp into ¼-inch pieces. Lightly salt tomato shells and turn upside down to drain for a few minutes. Preheat oven to 350°. Heat olive oil in a medium skillet over medium-low heat. Sauté onion for 4 to 5 minutes, or until soft but not brown. Add saffron, garlic and marjoram and cook for another minute. Stir in rice, chicken, tomato pulp and parsley and mix well. Season with salt and pepper. Divide stuffing among tomato halves. Place tomatoes in a lightly oiled shallow baking pan. Bake tomatoes until hot, about 15 minutes. Place on a serving platter and serve warm.

poultry

Sherried Chicken Wings

Oven-baked chicken wings are definitely finger food tapas that everyone will love. Serve with plenty of napkins. These marinate in the refrigerator for 3 to 4 hours before baking.

10 chicken wings, about 2 lb.
2 cloves garlic, coarsely chopped
2 tbs. full-flavored olive oil
2 tbs. honey
¼ cup cream sherry

1 tsp. paprika
½ tsp. dry mustard
a few drops Tabasco Sauce
½ tsp. salt
freshly ground pepper

❧ Prepare chicken wings. Cut each wing into 3 pieces. Reserve wing tips for the stockpot. Trim off any excess skin and fat from the drummette and wing piece. Wash and pat dry. Place chicken pieces in a zipper-top plastic bag. Combine garlic, oil, honey, sherry, paprika, mustard, Tabasco, salt and pepper. Pour over chicken pieces. Close bag and shake to distribute marinade, coating each piece. Refrigerate for 3 to 4 hours, turning bag occasionally.

❧ Preheat oven to 375°. Line a rimmed cookie sheet with aluminum foil. Spray a rack with nonstick cooking spray and place on foil. Remove chicken from marinade and arrange on baking rack. Discard marinade. Bake chicken for 25 minutes, turn pieces over and continue to bake until chicken is cooked through and nicely browned, about another 25 minutes. Serve immediately or refrigerate. Remove from refrigerator about 30 minutes before serving.

poultry

Lentil & Duck Salad

*If you have a local Chinese market or restaurant that roasts fresh ducks, buy half a duck for this salad. If roast duck is not available, substitute **Sherry-Glazed Sausage Chunks**, page 135, smoked chicken or ham. This salad can be made a day ahead and refrigerated.*

1 cup lentils, brown or green
2 cups water
2 whole cloves
1 onion, peeled, cut in half
1 bay leaf
3 carrots, peeled, cut into ⅛-inch dice, about 1 cup
3 tbs. full-flavored olive oil, divided
½ cup finely chopped onion

2 cloves garlic, finely chopped
¼ tsp. dried red pepper flakes
1 cup diced roasted duck meat, in ¼-inch dice
2 tbs. sherry or balsamic wine vinegar
½ tsp. salt
freshly ground pepper
¼ cup chopped fresh parsley

Pick over lentils, rinse and drain. Place in a medium saucepan with water. Stick a clove in each onion half and add to pan with bay leaf. Bring water to boil, reduce heat, cover and simmer for about 20 minutes. Start checking to see if lentils are tender but not mushy at 15 minutes. Do not overcook. Remove pan from heat, drain lentils in a sieve and place in a serving bowl. Discard onion, cloves and bay leaf. Bring 2 cups of water to a boil in a small saucepan. Blanch diced carrots for 2 to 3 minutes, or until crisp-tender. Drain and add to serving bowl.

Heat 1 tablespoon of the oil in a small skillet over medium-low heat. Sauté onion for 3 to 4 minutes, or until soft. Add garlic and red pepper flakes and cook for 1 minute. Add onion mixture and duck meat to serving bowl. Whisk together remaining 2 tablespoons of olive oil, vinegar, salt and pepper. Pour over warm lentils and gently toss to combine. Garnish with parsley. Serve warm or at room temperature.

poultry

meat *tapas*

Include at least one of these beef, lamb or pork dishes to create a nice balance at your next tapas table. Here are some delicious meat tapas to tempt you. Savory empanadas, flavorful *Meatballs (Albóndigas) in Almond Sherry Sauce*, *Sherry-Glazed Sausage Chunks*, and *Oven-Roasted Baby Back Ribs* all can be made ahead and reheated at the last moment.

For cooking ease and to reduce fat, *Lamb Meatballs in Tomato Sauce* are baked rather than fried, before being simmered in the sauce. *Roasted Pork Tenderloins* and *Prune and Olive Compote* are elegant and easy and any leftovers make great sandwiches. Good chorizo is sometimes hard to find, so we have included a flavorful homemade recipe. Use it to stuff mushroom caps or as a filling for quesadillas or tacos. A light fruity red or rose wine complements these hearty meat tapas.

Anticuchos

These zippy chunks of beef heart are really from Peru and Ecuador. If heart isn't available, top sirloin makes a nice substitute. The meat needs to marinate overnight, so prepare the day before. This dish goes well with beer or sangria.

2 lb. beef heart or sirloin steak
¾ cup red wine vinegar
2 tsp. dried red pepper flakes
1 tbs. paprika
2 cloves garlic, finely chopped
4 jalapeño peppers, stemmed, seeded and finely chopped

½ tsp. dried oregano
1 tbs. ground cumin
1 tsp. salt
2 tbs. olive oil
bamboo skewers

❧ Trim meat to remove any fat or veins, and cut into 1-inch cubes. Process vinegar, red pepper flakes, paprika, garlic, jalapeño, oregano, cumin, salt and oil with a food processor or in a blender bowl until smooth. Place meat cubes in a zipper-top plastic bag and pour marinade over meat. Exclude most of the air from the bag and close tightly. Place bag in refrigerator and marinate overnight, turning bag once or twice.

❧ If using bamboo skewers, soak in water for 30 minutes before using. When ready to grill, remove meat from refrigerator and allow to come to room temperature. Drain and reserve marinade. Skewer 4 or 5 chunks of meat on each skewer. Grill over hot coals or place under a preheated broiler, and grill for 2 to 3 minutes. Brush with reserved marinade, turn over and grill for an additional 1 to 2 minutes. The meat should be cooked until medium rare.

Note: Some health authorities discourage eating undercooked meat because of possible bacterial contamination.

meat

Beef & Potato Empanadas

Make these tender-crusted pies a day or two ahead and reheat them in the oven just before serving. Turkey, veal or lean pork can be substituted for ground beef if you like.

1 tbs. full-flavored olive oil
½ lb. ground round steak
¾ cup minced onion, 1 small
1 jalapeño pepper, stemmed, seeded and finely chopped
1 clove garlic, minced
1 small uncooked potato, peeled and cut into ¼-inch dice, about ½ cup
1 medium carrot, cut into ¼-inch dice

2 tsp. ground cumin
1 tbs. tomato paste
1 cup beef broth or water
1 tsp. salt
freshly ground black pepper
1 tbs. minced fresh cilantro
1 recipe *Basic Empanada Pastry*, page 148, or *Easy Empanada Pastry*, page 150

❧Heat oil in a medium skillet over high heat. Crumble beef into skillet and cut into small pieces with a spatula. Add onion, jalapeño and garlic. Cook, stirring until beef is cooked through, but not browned. Add potato, carrot, cumin and tomato paste, and stir to combine. Add broth, salt and pepper. Reduce heat to medium and simmer uncovered for 15 minutes, or until potatoes are tender. If there is any liquid remaining in bottom of pan, increase heat and cook until liquid has evaporated. Allow mixture to cool and stir in cilantro before filling empanada pastry. Assemble and bake empanadas as instructed in *Basic Empanada Pastry*.

Baked empanadas can be frozen. Preheat oven to 350°. Place frozen empanadas on a cookie sheet and bake until hot, about 15 to 20 minutes. If empanadas have been refrigerated, reheat until warm to the touch, about 7 to 10 minutes.

meat

Chorizo-Stuffed Mushroom Caps

• Makes about 20 pieces

Authentic Spanish chorizo is sometimes difficult to find in this country. Try easy homemade chorizo and use as filling for bite-sized mushrooms. Eat as finger food or serve on small plates with forks.

½ lb. lean ground pork
1 small clove garlic, finely chopped
1 tbs. prepared chili powder
¼ tsp. ground coriander
2 tbs. red wine vinegar
½ tsp. salt
generous grinds black pepper

20 (1½-inch) mushroom caps, brown or white
⅓ cup water
1 tbs. tomato paste
2 tbs. grated manchego or Parmesan cheese

❧ Combine pork, garlic, chili powder, coriander, vinegar, salt and pepper. Cover and refrigerate for 1 to 2 hours. While mixture is chilling, clean and trim mushroom caps. Twist out mushroom stems, chop finely and reserve. With a melon baller or small sharp spoon, enlarge mushroom cap stuffing area by digging out some of the gills.

❧ Remove meat from the refrigerator. Heat a medium skillet over medium heat. Crumble pork into skillet and add chopped mushroom stems. Stir as mixture browns and break into small pieces with a spatula. When browned, add water and tomato paste and continue to cook for 5 minutes, or until mixture is almost dry.

meat

122 TAPAS FANTÁSTICAS

Preheat oven to 375°. In a shallow baking pan large enough to hold mushrooms in one layer, add enough water to cover ½ inch of the bottom of the pan. Spoon a little of the stuffing mixture into each mushroom cap, pressing mixture down lightly but firmly. Sprinkle with cheese. Bake uncovered until mushroom caps are tender when pierced with the tip of a knife, about 20 minutes. Remove from liquid, drain on paper towels and arrange on a serving plate. Serve warm.

Chorizo-Stuffed Mushroom Caps

Lamb Meatballs in Tomato Sauce

These cilantro-scented meat-balls are browned in the oven and simmered in an aromatic tomato sauce. Make them ahead and reheat before serving. Serve with toothpicks or on small plates with forks.

2 tbs. medium amontillado sherry
½ cup fresh breadcrumbs
3 cloves garlic
¾ tsp. kosher salt
¾ lb. lean ground lamb
1 large egg
¼ cup finely minced onion
¼ cup finely chopped fresh cilantro leaves, plus some for garnish
½ tsp. ground cumin
¼ tsp. ground coriander
1 tsp. paprika

generous grinds of freshly ground pepper

Tomato Sauce
1 tbs. olive oil
½ cup finely chopped onion
1 tbs. flour
1 can (14 oz.) beef broth
2 tbs. tomato paste
½ tsp. ground cumin
2 tsp. Dijon mustard
fresh cilantro leaves for garnish

☙ Preheat oven to 450°. Line a large shallow baking pan or jelly-roll pan with aluminum foil. Spray foil with nonstick cooking spray. Add sherry to breadcrumbs and set aside to soak. Mince garlic on a cutting board and sprinkle salt on top. Use the side of your knife and reduce garlic to a paste. Place lamb in a mixing bowl. Add soaked breadcrumbs, garlic with egg, onion, cilantro, cumin, coriander, paprika and pepper. Mix until well combined. Form into 30 meatballs about 1¼ inches in diameter. Place meatballs on prepared baking sheet and bake until nicely browned, about 15 minutes.

meat

❧ While meatballs are browning, prepare the sauce. Heat oil in a heavy 3-quart saucepan. Sauté onion over medium-high heat for 4 to 5 minutes, or until lighty browned. Stir in flour and cook another minute. Add beef broth, tomato paste, cumin and mustard. Simmer for a few minutes until thick and smooth. Add browned meatballs to sauce and bring to a boil. Cover and simmer over very low heat for 30 minutes. Spoon into a serving bowl, garnish with fresh cilantro leaves and serve hot.

Lamb Meatballs in Tomato Sauce

Meatballs (Albóndigas) in Almond Sherry Sauce

Albóndigas are classic Spanish tapas. They are even better the next day so make them ahead and reheat before serving. Serve on small plates with a fork or with toothpicks.

¾ lb. ground veal
¾ lb. lean ground pork
1 cup finely chopped onion
3 cloves garlic, finely chopped
1 large egg, lightly beaten
½ cup fresh breadcrumbs

½ tsp. salt
½ tsp. freshly ground black pepper
¼ cup chopped fresh parsley, divided
flour for coating meatballs
3 tbs. olive oil

❧ Combine veal, pork, onion, garlic, egg, breadcrumbs, salt, pepper and 2 tablespoons of parsley. Mix well. Place flour on a large plate or pie pan. Form meat mixture into 1-inch meatballs and lightly roll each one in flour. Heat oil in a large skillet over medium-high heat. Lightly brown meatballs on all sides. Do this in 2 or 3 batches, depending on size of skillet. Remove browned meatballs to a plate with a slotted spoon and set aside.

meat

Almond Sherry Sauce

additional olive oil if needed
2 tbs. flour
½ cup finely ground almonds

1 can (14½ oz.) beef broth
⅓ cup dry sherry
salt and freshly ground pepper

❧ Heat same skillet used for meatballs. If necessary, add enough olive oil to make 3 tablespoons of liquid. Stir in flour and almonds and cook over medium-low heat for 1 to 2 minutes, but do not brown. Gradually stir in beef broth, sherry, salt and pepper, mixing well. Increase heat to medium and stir until sauce thickens. Reduce heat to low and add meatballs to sauce. Cover and simmer meatballs in sauce for 30 minutes, turning meatballs 2 or 3 times during cooking. If sauce becomes too thick, thin with a little water. Spoon into a heated bowl, sprinkle with remaining parsley just before serving and serve warm.

To keep meatballs warm during serving, place on a warming tray, or spoon into a small microwavable bowl and reheat in the microwave as needed.

meat

Roast Beef Rolls

Spread deli roast beef slices with your favorite blue-veined cheese for appetizing tapas. These can be made a day ahead and sliced just before serving.

2 oz. blue-veined cheese — cabrales, Roquefort, Maytag or Danish blue
2 oz. whipped cream cheese
generous grinds black pepper

6 oz. thin sliced roast beef, about 5 to 6 slices
2 tbs. finely chopped fresh parsley

❧ Combine blue and cream cheeses and mix well. Season with pepper. Spread a thin layer of cheese on each beef slice. Start from the small end and roll each slice up into a compact roll. Refrigerate until ready to serve. To serve, cut each roll into ¾-inch slices, wiping knife clean between cuts. Dip cut side of each roll into chopped parsley and arrange on a serving plate.

meat

Savory Pork Chunks

Cubes of tender braised pork are coated with spices and broiled briefly to give them a nice crusty coating. Serve hot with toothpicks.

1 lb. pork shoulder, trimmed of fat, cut into 1½-inch cubes
1 cup chicken broth
2 cloves garlic, peeled
1 tsp. tomato paste

1 tsp. sherry wine vinegar
1 tsp. paprika
½ tsp. kosher salt
⅛ tsp. cayenne pepper
freshly ground black pepper

❧ Trim surface fat from pork cubes and place in a saucepan. Add chicken broth and garlic. Bring to a boil, lower heat and simmer covered for 30 minutes. Remove pork from broth and place on a foil-lined baking pan. Discard garlic, skim fat from braising liquid and reduce over high heat to about ⅓ cup. Add tomato paste and sherry wine vinegar. Preheat broiler. Combine paprika, salt, cayenne and pepper. Sprinkle half of the spice mixture over the pork pieces. Place under broiler about 6 inches from heat source. Broil for 2 to 3 minutes, or until pork is lightly browned. Remove pork from broiler, turn pieces over and sprinkle them with remaining spice. Broil for 2 to 3 minutes until brown and crisp on the second side. Do not overcook. Reheat broth, add pork pieces and toss to coat with sauce. Pour into a serving dish.

meat

Oven-Roasted Baby Back Ribs

• Makes 6 to 8 servings

These delectable morsels take very little work and can be roasted ahead of time and heated just before serving. Cut them into individual ribs and serve as finger food.

2 racks baby back ribs, about 4 lb.
1 ½ tbs. paprika or mild New Mexico chile powder
1 ½ tsp. dry mustard powder
1 ½ tsp. ground coriander
1 ½ tsp. garlic powder
1 ½ tsp. ground cumin
1 ½ tsp. salt

½ tsp. freshly ground black pepper

Basting sauce
⅓ cup cream sherry
2 tbs. sherry wine vinegar
¼ tsp. Tabasco Sauce, or to taste
½ tsp. salt

❧Trim any surface fat from ribs. Combine paprika, mustard, coriander, garlic powder, cumin, salt and pepper. Sprinkle spice mixture evenly over both sides of ribs and gently massage into meat. Allow meat to stand at cool room temperature for 1 to 2 hours.

❧Preheat oven to 325°. Line a large baking sheet with aluminum foil. Place ribs meaty-side up on foil. Add ⅓ cup of water to pan. Loosely cover meat with another sheet of foil and bake for 1 hour. Remove foil, turn ribs over and continue to bake uncovered for 30 minutes. Pour off accumulated fat from pan and turn ribs over again. Continue to roast for another 40 to 45 minutes. Meat should be very tender and starting to pull away from the bone. Remove ribs from oven and cool.

meat

᪥ Combine cream sherry, wine vinegar, Tabasco and salt. Just before serving, preheat oven to 450°. Place ribs on a baking sheet. Brush with basting sauce or your favorite barbecue sauce and place in oven to heat through, about 15 minutes. Liberally baste with sauce and turn every few minutes. Cut into individual ribs for easy eating and serve immediately.

Oven-Roasted Baby Back Ribs

Roasted Pork Tenderloins

*Mustard-glazed pork tenderloins roast quickly. To serve, top thin slices of roasted pork with a little **Prune and Olive Compote**, page 133, or **Romesco** or **Parsley Sauce**, pages 142 and 144.*

2 pork tenderloins, about ¾ lb. each
2 tbs. Dijon mustard
2 tbs. honey
2 tbs. medium amontillado sherry

salt and freshly ground pepper
Prune and Olive Compote, page 133
watercress or parsley leaves for garnish

❧ Preheat oven to 400°. With a sharp knife, trim tenderloins of fat and silverskin. Combine mustard, honey and sherry. Spread half of the mustard mixture over each tenderloin. Place tenderloins on a rack in a baking pan. Roast pork until internal temperature reaches 160° on a meat thermometer, about 20 to 25 minutes. Remove from oven and allow to cool. To serve, slice into ½-inch medallions, top with a little *Prune and Olive Compote* and garnish with a watercress or parsley leaf. Serve at a cool room temperature.

meat

Prune and Olive Compote

Use this piquant mixture to top roast pork tenderloin slices or smoked ham squares. Or put a spoonful on top of a crisp cracker and spread with a little creamy goat cheese. This keeps for several days in the refrigerator

⅓ cup softened prunes
⅓ cup kalamata olives
1 tsp. sherry wine vinegar
1 tsp. Dijon mustard

1 tsp. brown sugar
salt and freshly ground pepper
2 tbs. chopped fresh cilantro
1 tbs. capers, drained and rinsed

❧ Remove pits from prunes and olives and chop them into small pieces on a chopping board. Place mixture into a small bowl and add vinegar, mustard, sugar, a little salt and pepper. Stir well. Spread a small amount of mixture on each pork slice. Garnish with a cilantro leaf and 1 or 2 capers.

meat

Veal, Raisin & Pine Nut Empanadas

A cinnamon and allspice flavored filling give these flaky empanadas a Moorish touch. Cool mixture before filling empanada pastry.

1 tbs. full-flavored olive oil
½ lb. lean ground veal
1 cup finely chopped onion, about 1 medium
¼ tsp. cinnamon
⅛ tsp. allspice
½ tsp. salt

½ cup water
2 tbs. amontillado sherry or brandy
¼ cup golden raisins, coarsely chopped
¼ cup toasted pine nuts
1 recipe *Basic Empanada Pastry*, page 148, or *Easy Empanada Pastry*, page 150

❧ Heat oil in a medium skillet over medium heat. Crumble in veal and break up large pieces with a spatula. Add onion and continue to cook until veal is cooked through. Add cinnamon, allspice and salt, and stir to combine. Add water, sherry and raisins. Continue cooking for 15 minutes, or until moisture has completely evaporated. Remove from heat and cool. Stir in pine nuts.

❧ Assemble and bake empanadas as instructed in the *Basic Basic Empanada Pastry*.

Baked empanadas can be frozen. Preheat oven to 350°. Place frozen empanadas on cookie sheet and bake until hot, about 15 to 20 minutes. If empanadas have been refrigerated, reheat until warm to the touch, about 7 to 10 minutes.

meat

Sherry-Glazed Sausage Chunks

Fully cooked sausages such as Polish or kielbasa can be used without poaching. Italian, garlic and other raw sausages must be poached before slicing and cooking in sherry.

1 lb. cooked sausage — kielbasa, Polish, chorizo or linguiça

½ cup cream sherry

❧ Cut sausages into ¾-inch pieces. Pour sherry into skillet, add sausages and cook over medium-high heat for 4 to 5 minutes, or until sherry evaporates and sausages are lightly browned. Stir frequently during cooking. Serve warm with toothpicks.

Sausages can be cooked and reheated in the microwave for 1 minute before serving.

Fresh Sausage Variation: For fresh, uncooked Italian sausages, turkey or other specialty sausages, poach sausages first in water. See method in *Sausages & Figs in Orange Sherry Sauce*, see page 136.

meat

Sausages & Figs in Orange Sherry Sauce

Dried Calimyrna or Mission figs pair deliciously with sausage cooked in a little orange juice and sherry. Make ahead of time, and reheat just before serving. Serve warm on small plates or with toothpicks.

1 lb. uncooked mild Italian
   sausages
1 cup water
1 medium onion, thinly sliced
zest and juice from 1 orange

⅓ cup medium amontillado sherry
1 tsp. sherry wine vinegar
8 oz. dried Calimyrna figs, stemmed, cut
   in half or quarters
generous grinds black pepper

❧ Place sausages in a medium skillet with water. Bring to a boil, cover, lower heat and simmer for 8 to 10 minutes, turning sausages over halfway during cooking. Drain and discard liquid from skillet. Increase heat to medium-high. Cook sausages, turning frequently for 2 to 3 minutes, or until lightly browned on both sides. Remove sausages from skillet and place on a cutting board. Add onion to skillet and cook over medium heat for 2 minutes. Add orange juice and zest, sherry, wine vinegar and figs to skillet. Cover and cook for 2 minutes, or until figs are softened. Cut sausages into ¾-inch slices and add to skillet. Cover and cook for 2 more minutes. Uncover, increase heat to high and reduce liquid in pan to about ¼ cup. Turn sausages into a heated serving dish and finish with a generous grind of black pepper. Serve hot.

meat

Sausages & Figs in Orange Sherry Sauce, page 136

basic sauces & pastry

Sauces add vivid color, texture and complementary flavors to simply pre-pared foods. Romesco and tomato sauces are probably the most widely used in Spain, followed by the garlicky, mayonnaise-based aïoli. Prepare one or two of these sauces, keep them refrigerated, and serve with steamed veg-etables, grilled meats or seafood. Taste the magic that these sauces will add to the foods on your tapas table.

Empanadas and tartaletas are also served on the tapas table. Here are two empanada pastries, a traditional crust and an *Easy Empanada Pastry* that requires no chilling. Both can be made in the food processor, have excellent flavor and are easy to handle.

Aïoli

• MAKES 1 CUP

This is a sauce for garlic lovers. Serve it with grilled vegetables or fish, **Fried Calamari,** *page 84,* **Roasted Baby Potatoes with Garlic***, page 73, or as a base for bruschetta toppings. Mash the garlic with salt in a mortar with a pestle or put it through a garlic press to get it very fine.*

4 to 5 cloves garlic
½ tsp. kosher or coarse salt
1 cup prepared mayonnaise

2 tsp. lemon juice
2 tbs. full-flavored olive oil
⅛ tsp. white pepper

Peel garlic cloves, coarsely chop and place in a mortar with salt. Crush garlic with pestle until very smooth. If you have a large mortar, add mayonnaise, lemon juice, olive oil and pepper to garlic and mix until well combined. Otherwise scrape crushed garlic into a small bowl, add remaining ingredients and whisk until well combined. Refrigerate if not using immediately.

basics

Almond Sauce

Serve this quick versatile sauce with cooked asparagus, green beans, steamed new potatoes or broccoli, grilled fish, or with **Velvet Chicken Breast Chunks***, page 111. This sauce tends to thicken when refrigerated. Add more chicken broth or water to thin it before serving.*

½-¾ cup chicken broth
3 tbs. chopped shallots
1 cup (about 3 oz.) almond slices, toasted
2 tbs. lemon juice

2 tbs. dry sherry
1 tsp. sherry wine vinegar
2 tbs. full-flavored olive oil
salt and freshly ground pepper
paprika for garnish

❧ Bring ½ cup chicken broth and shallots to a boil in a small saucepan. Cook 3 to 4 minutes, or until shallots are softened. Remove from heat. Place almonds in a food processor bowl and process until mixture resembles coarse meal. With motor running, add lemon juice, sherry, wine vinegar, oil, chicken broth and shallots. Process until well combined. Season with salt and pepper. Thin sauce with more chicken broth, if needed, to produce a pourable sauce. Sprinkle with paprika. Spoon over vegetables or fish, or serve in individual dishes and use as a dipping sauce.

basics

Parsley Sauce

• MAKES ⅔ CUP

*Serve this piquant green sauce with **Steamed Mussels with Parsley Sauce**, page 95, **Steamed Clams**, page 87, grilled seafood, chicken or sausages. This keeps in the refrigerator for 3 or 4 days.*

2 cloves garlic ,peeled
2 green onions, white part only, cut into
    1-inch lengths
⅓ cup full-flavored olive oil
¼ cup capers, rinsed, drained and dried
1 tbs. anchovy paste, or 3 anchovy fillets,
    oil-packed

2 tsp. Dijon mustard
2 tsp. sherry wine vinegar
½ tsp. sugar
⅛ tsp. white pepper
⅓ cup fresh finely chopped Italian
    parsley, tightly packed
salt

❧ In a food processor bowl with the motor running, drop garlic and onion pieces through feed tube and process until finely chopped. Scrape down sides of bowl. Add oil, capers, anchovy, mustard, vinegar, sugar and pepper. Process until smooth. Add parsley and pulse 2 to 3 times to combine. Add salt to taste. Refrigerate until ready to serve.

basics

Red Pepper Mayonnaise

• MAKES ½ CUP

This vibrant red sauce accents any cold seafood or chicken dish.

½ cup prepared mayonnaise
¼ cup roasted red pepper pieces

¼ tsp. paprika
1 tbs. brandy or cognac

❧ Place ingredients in a blender or food processor bowl and process until smooth. Chill until ready to use.

basics

Romesco Sauce

Serve this Spanish sauce with hot grilled shrimp, scallops, chicken, baby leeks or green onions. It is also delicious in quesadillas, ham or roast beef sandwiches. Make it 2 or 3 days ahead of time, and refrigerate until ready to serve.

½ cup full-flavored olive oil, divided
2 slices French-style bread, ½-inch thick, crusts removed
2 large red bell peppers
1 small onion, peeled, cut into ½-inch slices
3 cloves garlic, peeled

2 tomatoes
¼ tsp. dried red pepper flakes
1 tsp. paprika
⅓ cup toasted almonds
2 tbs. red wine vinegar
2 tbs. water
salt and freshly ground pepper

❧ Heat 1 tablespoon of the oil in a medium skillet over medium heat. Sauté bread on both sides until nicely browned. Remove bread, cut into 3 or 4 pieces and reserve. Preheat broiler. Line a shallow baking pan with foil. Place red peppers, onion slices and garlic on foil. Cut tomatoes in half and remove cores and seeds. Place in baking pan cut-sides down. Brush vegetables with olive oil and broil about 8 inches from heat source for 8 to 10 minutes. Turn vegetables as they begin to char and continue to cook for 5 to 7 minutes, or until soft. Remove peppers, wrap in foil and allow to steam for 10 minutes.

❧ Pull off skin from peppers, discard seeds, core and chop coarsely. Place peppers in a food processor bowl with onions, garlic and tomatoes. Add bread pieces, red pepper flakes, paprika, almonds, wine vinegar, water and remaining olive oil. Process until smooth. Season with salt and pepper. Refrigerate for 30 minutes before serving. The sauce should be the consistency of heavy cream; stir in a little water if it gets too thick.

basics

Seafood Cocktail Sauce

• MAKES ¾ CUP

Serve this zesty sauce with boiled shrimp, grilled scallops, Shrimp A La Plancha, page 102, Calamari Cocktail, page 85, or Fried Calamari, page 84.

¾ cup bottled chili sauce
1 tbs. creamy horseradish
1 tbs. lemon juice

½ tsp. brown sugar
salt and freshly ground pepper

∾ Combine chili sauce with horseradish, lemon juice, brown sugar, salt and pepper. Use immediately or refrigerate for several days.

Sherry Vinegar & Shallot Sauce

Spoon this shallot-laced sauce over steamed clams or fresh oysters.

⅓ cup sherry wine vinegar

3 small shallots, finely chopped

salt and freshly ground pepper

❧ Combine ingredients in an attractive small bowl and serve with prepared shellfish.

basics

Spicy Tomato Sauce

This sauce eclipses any ketchup. Serve it warm with **Spciy Baked Potato Wedges**, *page 74,* **Mini-Tortillas**, *page 48, boiled or grilled shrimp,* **Fried Calamari**, *page 84, or just spoon it on a grilled hamburger.*

1 tbs. olive oil
½ cup very finely chopped onions
3 to 4 large cloves garlic, finely minced
½ cup dry red wine
2 tbs. red wine vinegar
1 can (8 oz.) tomato sauce

2 tbs. tomato paste
1 tsp. paprika
1 tsp. brown sugar
⅛ tsp. cayenne pepper or salt to taste
Tabasco Sauce, optional

❧ Heat oil and onions in a small heavy saucepan over medium heat. Reduce heat and cook onion for 4 to 5 minutes or until translucent and soft, but not brown. Add garlic and cook for another minute. Add wine and vinegar to pan, bring to a boil and cook over high heat for 2 to 3 minutes. Add tomato sauce and paste, paprika, sugar and cayenne. Bring to a boil, reduce heat to low and simmer for 15 minutes, or until sauce thickens slightly. Stir frequently during cooking. Taste carefully and add more cayenne or some Tabasco, if desired.

basics

Basic Empanada Pastry

This traditional tender, flaky pastry is perfect for any empanada filling. It requires an hour in the refrigerator before rolling and cutting.

3 cups all-purpose flour
1 tsp. salt
½ cup cold vegetable shortening, butter or lard, cut into cubes

2 large eggs
3 to 4 tbs. ice water
1 egg white for glaze

❧ Place flour and salt in a food processor bowl. Pulse a few times to combine. Add shortening and pulse several times until mixture resembles coarse meal. With processor running, add enough ice water until dough forms a ball. Divide dough in half, flatten into disks about ¾-inch thick, wrap in plastic wrap and refrigerate for at least 1 hour before rolling and cutting the dough.

❧ Place dough between 2 sheets of waxed paper and roll out to a thickness of ⅛-inch. Cut as many 2¾-inch or 4-inch circles from the dough as possible. Combine dough scraps, roll out again and cut more circles.

❧ Preheat oven to 375°. Line a cookie sheet with parchment paper. Place a slightly rounded teaspoon of filling for small empanadas, or about 2 tablespoons of filling for larger empanadas, on the bottom half of each pastry circle. Brush edge of dough with a little water to help seal. Fold dough over to form a half-circle and press edges firmly together. Use fork tines to crimp the edges of each empanada. Place on prepared cookie sheet. Whisk egg

basics

white until foamy and brush on top of each empanada. Prick tops in 2 or 3 places with a fork to allow steam to escape. Bake until pastry is firm and lightly browned, about 25 minutes. Serve warm or at room temperature.

Baked empanadas can be frozen. Preheat oven to 350°. Place frozen empanadas on a cookie sheet and bake until hot, about 15 to 20 minutes. If empanadas have been refrigerated, reheat until warm to the touch, about 7 to 10 minutes.

Basic Empanada Pastry

Easy Empanada Pastry

This pastry goes together quickly, requires no chilling and is easy to roll out.

3 cups all-purpose flour
1 tsp. salt
1 tsp. baking powder
1 tsp. Spanish paprika
2 large eggs and 1 egg, separated

½ cup full-flavored olive oil
2 tbs. chilled fino or medium dry sherry, page 156
3 to 4 tbs. ice water

❧ Place flour, salt, baking powder and paprika in a food processor bowl. Pulse 1 to 2 times to combine. Add 1 whole egg, 1 egg yolk and olive oil to processor, and process until combined. Reserve second egg white to glaze empanadas. Add sherry and 3 tablespoons of the ice water and process for a few more seconds. Mixture will resemble coarse meal and hold together when pinched between thumb and forefinger. Add a few more drops of ice water if necessary.

❧ Preheat oven to 375°. Line a cookie sheet with parchment paper. Divide dough into 2 equal pieces and roll each piece between 2 pieces of plastic wrap to a thickness of ⅛-inch. Cut as many 2¾-inch circles from the dough as possible. Combine dough scraps, roll out again and cut more circles. Place a slightly rounded teaspoon of filling for small empanadas, or about 2 tablespoons of filling for larger empanadas on the bottom half of each pastry circle. Lightly brush bottom edge of dough with a little water to help seal. Fold dough over to form a half-circle and press edges firmly together. Use fork tines to crimp the edges of each empanada. Place on prepared cookie sheet. Whisk remaining egg white until foamy and brush on top of each empanada. Prick tops with a fork in 2 or 3 places to allow steam to escape. Bake until pastry is firm and lightly browned, about 25 minutes. Serve warm or at room temperature.

Baked empanadas can be frozen. Preheat oven to 350°. Place frozen empanadas on a cookie sheet and bake until hot, about 15 to 20 minutes. If empanadas have been refrigerated, reheat until warm to the touch, about 7 to 10 minutes.

Easy Empanada Pastry

Basic Tartlet Pastry

*Use these flaky shells for **Eggplant & Tomato Tartlets**, page 59, or **Tuna & Egg Tartlets**, page 107, or with your favorite filling. These small tartaletas or pastry shells are nice to have on hand, and will keep for several days when stored in an airtight container or kept frozen.*

1½ cups all-purpose flour
½ tsp. salt
8 tbs. (1 stick) chilled, unsalted butter,
   cut into 8 pieces

4 to 5 tbs. chilled dry sherry or ice water

❧ Place flour and salt in food processor bowl and pulse once or twice to mix well. Add butter and process until mixture resembles coarse meal. Sprinkle 4 tablespoons sherry on dough and pulse several times until mixture starts to form a ball. Add a few more drops of liquid if necessary to make dough hold together. Remove dough from processor and press into a flat rectangle. Wrap with plastic wrap and refrigerate for 1 hour.

❧ Preheat oven to 375°. Lightly oil back of 1 muffin pan and inside of another pan of the same size. Roll out chilled dough to ⅛-inch thickness. Use a small fluted cookie cutter to cut circles about ½-inch larger than diameter of tart pans. Gently press dough onto oiled back pan and top with another pan, pressing down firmly. Prick bottom of pastry cups with a fork. Bake for 15 minutes, remove top pan and return shells to oven to bake until shells are lightly browned and feel dry to the touch, about 3 more minutes. Cool both pans and repeat with remaining pastry dough. Cool baked shells and fill as directed.

Note: Chill dough for 1 hour before rolling out. Prebake shells by pressing the tart pastry on back of miniature muffin cups. Cover the pastry with another same size miniature muffin cup pan, and press pan down firmly on top of pastry.

basics

what do you drink with
tapas?

Sangria, page 158

The whole concept of tapas originated in Andalusia, Spain, the home of sherry. It is no coincidence that dry sherry pairs marvelously with classic Spanish tapas. Sherry wine production was well established before the time of Columbus, who included casks of it in the provisions for his voyages to the New World.

Wines labeled "sherry" are produced in many countries. Australia and South Africa produce some interesting sweet sherries, but the sherries most often found in the United States are from Spain, California and a few from New York.

The sherries preferred by Spaniards to go with tapas are light and dry. Lightest of all sherries are the manzanillas. Aged in the cooler, more humid climate of San Lucar de Barrameda, manzanillas tend to be lower in alcohol with a fresh, clean and slightly bitter taste. Manzanillas do not age well, so purchase them from a high volume merchant, store in the refrigerator and consume soon after purchase. Some excellent Spanish manzanilla and dry fino sherries are produced under Emlio Lustau, Duff Gordon, Hartley & Gibson, Gonzales Byass and Osborne labels.

Fino, aged in Jerez, which is inland from the coast, has a little more body and character than man-zanilla. Finos often are slightly fortified with brandy to give them a longer shelf life. They are at their best when served chilled with tapas.

Amontillado sherry is heavier and has been aged longer than manzanilla or fino. It is often forti-fied to bring the alcohol level up to 18 to 20 percent and sometimes is lightly sweetened. Amontillados are rich and full-bodied and are a little too powerful to accompany seafood tapas. They do pair well with tapas that contain meat or poultry in a distinctive sauce, particularly those containing garlic and tomatoes. Cream sherries are rich and sweet and are best saved for dessert.

American sherries are very well made and quite enjoyable. The ones that go best with tapas are labeled "fino" and often "dry sherry." They are rarely as light and dry as those from Spain. Wines with 18 percent or less alcohol will be less cloying and pair better with tapas. In California, Sheffield Cellars and Paul Masson produce a full range of sherries.

Sparkling wines are always festive, and go very well with a whole range of tapas. Spain produces wonderful cavas, wines made by the same method as the true French champagnes. They are less expensive than their French counterparts and readily available. Look for Freixenet or Codorniu.

what do you drink with
tapas?

California sparkling wines are also very good. Unless your budget demands, avoid the least expensive, bulk process, California sparklers. Spending just a few more dollars makes a world of difference in quality. Look for Mumm's, Chandon, Piper-Sonoma, Roderer Estate and Schramsberg.

Young fruity wines — white, red and especially rosé — are also suitable for tapas. A tapas party is not the occasion to serve fine old wines. Tapas party foods generally have assertive flavors that might overpower fine vintages. Look for inexpensive, young wines from Spain, California, Italy or the south of France. White, rosé, red Zinfandel or a crisp Sauvignon blanc from California are especially complimentary with tapas flavors.

The three major table wine-producing areas of Spain are the Rioja, Penedes and Valdepenas. Of these, Penedes produces a broader range of wines that go well with tapas. Look for the well-made wines of Miguel Torres, which are also widely available.

Beer is also a favorite with tapas. Many of the lagers and lighter ales produced by microbreweries are great with tapas. Avoid heavier, maltier and sweeter ales.

Sangria

Sangria has a gorgeous red-orange color and is typically made from red wine, fruit juices, sliced fruits and sparkling water. Sometimes a small amount of brandy or other liqueur is added. This refreshing drink is served over ice. Use an inexpensive Spanish wine or a California Zinfandel or Burgundy.

2 oranges, divided
1 bottle (750 ml.) young fruity red wine
1 ripe peach, sliced, or 1 cup frozen peach slices
¼ cup brandy, preferably Spanish or Mexican

2 tbs. sugar
1½ cups club soda
ice cubes for glasses
1 orange, thinly sliced for glasses
fruit for glasses
Triple Sec or orange liqueur, optional

∾ Chill all ingredients before combining with ice. Wash oranges. Thinly slice 1 orange and squeeze juice from second orange. Combine orange slices and juice, red wine, peaches, brandy and sugar in a large pitcher or nonreactive container. Stir until sugar is dissolved and refrigerate. Just before serving, add club soda and stir gently to combine. Place a few ice cubes in tall glasses and pour sangria over ice. Make certain everyone gets a slice each of orange and peach in a glass. If you like, float a little Triple Sec or orange liqueur on top of each glass before serving.

drinks

Limonada or Sangria Blanca

Limonada is not typically Spanish. It is a New World invention, but it makes a great accompaniment for tapas, especially in warm weather. Use a young, inexpensive white wine such as a Riesling, Chenin Blanc or other fruity wine. Regular frozen lemonade concentrate works well, but we particularly like to use the frozen raspberry-flavored lemonade.

1 bottle (750 ml.) fruity white wine
½ cup defrosted, undiluted frozen
   raspberry lemonade concentrate
1 lemon, washed, unpeeled and thinly
   sliced
½ cup vodka, optional

16 oz. club soda
1 cup raspberries
ice cubes for glasses
1 lemon, thinly sliced for glasses
additional raspberries for glasses

❧ Chill all ingredients. Combine white wine, raspberry lemonade, lemon and vodka in a pitcher or large bowl. Add chilled soda and raspberries just before serving and stir gently to combine. Place a few ice cubes in tall glasses and pour Limonda over ice. Make certain that everyone gets a lemon slice and a few raspberries in a glass.

drinks

what do you drink with
tapas?

margaritas

Classic Mexican margaritas go very well with a wide range of tapas. The best margaritas are prepared with tequila, freshly squeezed lime juice and a good quality orange liqueur. It isn't necessary to use aged golden tequila in your margaritas. The lime and orange liqueur flavors dominate and overpower the subtle complexity of finer tequilas. The commonly available Persian limes are fine in margaritas, but if you can find the smaller, paler green Mexican limes or Key limes — they are even better. Cointreau, while more expensive, has a more intense orange flavor and makes a better margarita than Triple Sec.

Classic Margarita

Be careful with these! They go down easily, but pack a real punch. After the second one, you might lose some of your guests.

2 oz. tequila
1 oz. Cointreau or Triple Sec
1 oz. freshly squeezed lime juice

crushed ice
kosher salt for glass rims

Shaker Margarita

❧ Pour tequila, Cointreau, lime juice and crushed ice in a cocktail shaker. Shake vigorously for 10 seconds and strain into a salt-rimmed margarita or martini glass.

Blender Margarita

❧ Double ingredients and place tequila, Cointreau, lime juice and 1 cup of crushed ice into blender bowl. Blend for a few seconds on high and pour into 2 salt-rimmed glasses.

Note: To make salt-rimmed glasses, pour a small amount of kosher or coarse salt on a piece of waxed paper or into a saucer. Rub the rim of each glass with a small piece of lime to moisten and roll rim in the salt.

Pitcher Margaritas

Pitcher margaritas are subtler and less alcoholic than the **Classic Margarita,** *page 161. Start with a good quality margarita mix, either frozen or bottled.*

∾ Combine margarita mix and tequila in the proportions directed on the mix, using the lesser amount of tequila if there is a range. Instead of water, add club soda to equal the amount of margarita mix and tequila to the pitcher just before serving. Stir gently and pour or ladle into tall salt-rimmed glasses over ice cubes.

drinks

Sherry Shrub

Shrubs have been around since revolutionary times. They are often made with rum, but also with brandy or sherry, and provide a refreshing tall drink to accompany tapas.

1 bottle (25 oz.) dry fino sherry, imported or domestic
⅓ cup undiluted frozen orange juice concentrate
2 tbs. Cointreau or Triple Sec
2 tbs. rum

2 tbs. lemon juice
3 cups club soda
ice for glasses
1 orange, thinly sliced for glasses
1 lemon, thinly sliced for glasses

❧ Mix sherry, orange juice, Cointreau, rum and lemon juice in a large pitcher, punchbowl or nonreactive container. Refrigerate drink until ready to serve. Just before serving, add chilled club soda and stir gently to combine. Place a few ice cubes in tall glasses, add an orange and lemon slice and pour drink over ice.

drinks

tapas
index

index

index

index

index

index

index

tapas
notes

tapas
notes

_____

_____

_____

_____

_____

_____

_____

_____

_____

_____

_____

_____

_____

_____

_____

_____

tapas
notes

_____

_____

_____

_____

_____

_____

_____

_____

_____

_____

_____

_____

_____

_____

_____

_____

_____

_____